The Working Woman's
Dream
Kitchen

The Working Woman's Dream Kitchen

Hilde Gabriel Lee

BETTERWAY PUBLICATIONS, INC.
WHITE HALL, VIRGINIA

Published by Betterway Publications, Inc.
P.O. Box 219
Crozet, VA 22932
(804) 823-5661

Cover design by Susan Riley
Cover photographs of Solarian Supreme, Designer Solarian II,
    and Designer Solarian courtesy of Armstrong World Industries, Inc.
Lower right photograph courtesy of Lili Lihn
Typography by East Coast Typography, Inc.

Library of Congress Cataloging-in-Publication Data

Lee, Hilde Gabriel.
    The working woman's dream kitchen / by Hilde Gabriel Lee.
        p.   cm.
    Includes index.
    ISBN 1-55870-173-7 : $14.95
    1. Kitchens–Design and construction. 2. Kitchen utensils.
    I. Title.
    TX653.L44 1990
    643'.3–dc20   90-39081
                                                        CIP

Printed in the United States of America
0 9 8 7 6 5 4 3 2 1

Contents

Introduction

Every cook and homemaker at some time in her life has dreamed of having the perfect kitchen. However, as styles of life and decoration change, and new appliances appear, so do our dreams change. Turning dreams into reality has become a major industry. According to the National Kitchen and Bath Association, over five and a half million kitchens are built or remodeled each year.

Over the years, I have had a number of kitchens, each better, more efficient, and more luxurious than the previous one. A year and a half ago, my husband and I built a home with my latest dream kitchen, but I have already found new appliances that I wish I had. Some I have added; others, which involve structural changes in the kitchen, will eventually be added. For me, dreaming about making improvements to my kitchen is a never ending activity.

My interest in cooking and kitchens stems from thirty years of homemaking experience, ten years of operating my own interior decorating business, and about the same period of time as a professional food columnist and cookbook writer. I have always loved to cook and experiment with new recipes. Having the right tools and facilities, in the right places, has become a necessity for me. This has forced me to be conscious of the design of my kitchen and how it can be improved.

A dream kitchen is not a stereotyped plan with pre-determined appliances, sinks, and cabinets. The dream kitchen is the total environment in which you desire to spend your cooking and possibly eating hours. You have to design it to fit your psychic as well as physical needs, whether you cook occasionally or a great deal. Any dream kitchen should conform to your lifestyle.

With today's lifestyles, kitchens are not confined to meal preparation alone. Typically, they have become the center of family activities. The kitchen is the place for family gatherings, informal entertaining, and other non-cooking activities. Thus, the dream kitchen can also become the family's dream.

Since kitchens are designed to suit individuals and their needs, I have tried in this book to present information that will assist you in formulating your dream kitchen. Realizing that there is a continuous flow of technology and new products for our kitchens, I have tried to provide the latest in new ideas and products.

I have occasionally inserted my own experiences regarding a style, product, or theory in the book. I hope they may help in planning your kitchen.

The history of food and cooking has always been of interest to me and I have, therefore, devoted the first chapter of this book to the history of the kitchen in the United States. This provides a good background for the design of your modern kitchen with all its conveniences.

The next three chapters are concerned with the basic use of the kitchen, the major work areas, and the most popular kitchen designs. Chapters 5, 6, and 7 provide overviews of the major kitchen appliances, including the latest innovations.

The chapter on cabinets presents a variety of

storage ideas, and the following chapter gives an overview of the types of materials that can be used in a kitchen. Chapter 10 briefly reviews trends in kitchen decor, and the last two chapters discuss the myriad of small appliances and cooking aids.

I have chosen not to include special layout tools for kitchen design since there are a number of useful books and magazines on the market containing these practical tools.

I have avoided presenting price comparisons in this book, since prices for similar products vary among manufacturers and prices for construction and installation of appliances vary in different parts of the country. I have avoided making judgments about one product versus another, since everyone has different likes, dislikes, and needs. One appliance may suit one individual and not another. I have, however, tried to identify the major product features on the market today.

All of the manufacturers included in the book are well-established in the marketplace and back their products with appropriate warranties. This does not mean to imply that manufacturers I have not mentioned are not equally well-established.

I wish to thank all of the manufacturers who so graciously supplied information and pictorial assistance for this book. Although not every manufacturer in every aspect of kitchen products is represented in this book, there is a good cross-section of them which will give the reader basic and new product information. I also want to thank my husband, Allan, for his encouragement and valuable assistance in the preparation of this book.

How to Use This Book

The Working Woman's Dream Kitchen is a reference book for those who desire to remodel an existing kitchen or build a new kitchen. It covers kitchen plans, major kitchen appliances, cabinets, materials used in a kitchen, small appliances, and cookware. The book should alleviate some of your preliminary shopping by providing information to help you, the busy working woman, formulate ideas for your dream kitchen. It will make you more knowledgeable when you do start shopping and will help narrow down the number of choices you face.

A recent *New York Times* survey asked working women how much time they spend in preparing the evening meal and how much time they would like to spend. The results showed that most women spend sixty minutes, but would rather spend twenty minutes. With this in mind, many women are either changing appliances, remodeling their kitchens, or purchasing new homes with more efficient kitchens. According to the National Kitchen and Bath Association, 5.9 million kitchens will be remodeled or built in 1990.

In my discussions with working women who prepare meals, I have found that there are basically three types of family cooks: (A) those who find cooking a chore; (B) those who like to cook, but find little time to do so; and (C) those who love to cook and find ways to spend significant time in the kitchen. The A type of family cook does not need as extensive a kitchen as does a type-C cook.

To help the reader make use of this book, I have developed typical profiles of cooking habits within each category. I have also profiled several variations within each category, since individual needs vary depending on the family's lifestyle. At the end of the profiles there is a chart that identifies the aspects of kitchen change each women in my survey desires and where in this book she could find helpful information regarding desired changes.

First, there is the working woman, let's call her Ann, who cooks for a family of two and who does not spend a great deal of time in the kitchen. For her, cooking is a chore and her busy schedule leaves little time for meal preparation. Ann often stops on the way home and picks up semi-prepared food, like marinated chicken breasts or barbecued ribs. Her husband helps with some of the food preparation and often prepares the salad, as well as does the barbecuing in the summer months. Since there are only two in Ann's family, she prepares quick and simple meals, and they often eat out, so she does not need a large kitchen. A kitchen of about 100 to 120 square feet with 8 to 10 feet of counter space serves her purpose well. Her dream is to add a second preparation sink and an island or peninsula for informal eating.

Amy, Ann's friend, also spends a limited time in the kitchen. There are four in Amy's family — her husband and two small children. Amy's children are fussy eaters; her husband prefers meat and potatoes; and Amy is into health foods and low-calorie meals. Amy wants a larger kitchen, about 200 square feet, where there is a definite informal eating area. Since there is such a variety in the types of foods Amy must prepare quickly, she uses a lot of frozen ingredients and prepares frozen entrées. Amy is not able to shop for groceries every day and wishes she had a refrigerator with more freezer space. Also she would like to have more cabinets.

Alice, a working mother with grown children, is involved in her work as well as her church and community activities. She does not have very much time to cook and likes to have dinner ready when her husband gets home a short time after she does. Consequently, Alice does some cooking ahead on the weekends and freezes a lot of entrées. Alice wants to have a 200 square foot kitchen and combine it with the family room so that they will have more eating and entertaining space for children, grandchildren, and friends.

Name	Interest	Reference
Ann	Second sink	Chapter 7 — Sinks
	Island for eating	Chapter 3 — Peninsulas and Islands
Amy	Informal eating area	Chapter 2 — The Eat-in Kitchen
	Refrigerator/freezer	Chapter 6 — Types of Refrigerators, Features, Storage
	Cabinets	Chapter 8 — Cabinets
	Cooktop	Chapter 5 — Cooktops
Alice	Kitchen–Family Room	Chapter 2 — The "Keeping Room" Kitchen
	Crock pot	Chapter 11 — Crock Pots
	Pressure cooker	Chapter 12 — Pressure Cookers

Our second group of working women starts with Betty, who is a nurse and works different shifts. She and her husband have two teenage sons who are not always present for meals and who like to prepare their own food in the microwave. How-

ever, there are many occasions when both of the boys want to use the microwave oven at the same time. Betty thinks a toaster oven and a new appliance she has heard about that cooks hot dogs, which both boys dearly love, might help solve the problem. With three men in the family, who prefer grilled meats, Betty wants to alter her kitchen to include a new cooktop and a separate built-in grill. She also needs more freezer space. Betty thinks she needs approximately 300 square feet in her kitchen, including the family eating area, to accommodate her cooking and storage needs.

Barbara has two teenage daughters, one who loves to cook and the other who loves to bake. Many times they start dinner or even prepare the entire meal for their working mother. For the past eight months there has been continuous discussion of remodeling the kitchen to suit not only Barbara, but also the girls. The daughter who likes to bake wants a convection oven; the other girl who does most of the food preparation wants a new food processor that will whip egg whites. Also, Barbara has been trying to decide what material to use for the floor of their kitchen. She would like to add another 50 square feet to her 250 square foot kitchen to accommodate the additional counter and storage space for her daughters.

Name	Interest	Reference
Betty	Toaster Oven	Chapter 12 — Toaster ovens
	Indoor grill	Chapter 5 — Indoor grills
Barbara	Convection oven	Chapter 5 — Convection ovens
	Floor material	Chapter 9 — Vinyl, marble, wood, carpet, ceramic tile
	Baking center	Chapter 3 — Baking area
	Food processor	Chapter 12 — Food Processors

The third group of working women is composed of avid cooks. They love to collect cookbooks and try new recipes. They also entertain quite often. Cathy has a 200 square foot kitchen with an eating area where she and her husband eat most of their meals, since there are only two in the family. Cathy's kitchen does not have an effective work triangle, and she finds it very inefficient. She has a center island with a sink and cabinets along the two walls facing the sink. One wall houses the cooktop and the other the refrigerator. She has only one built-in oven. Cathy wants to install a double oven. She wants to expand her kitchen and create an efficient work triangle.

Carol, who also loves to cook, wants a place in her kitchen where she can store some of her cookbooks and also do some of her meal planning, since she entertains at least once a month. Her husband wants a designated place in the kitchen to prepare drinks for the guests. Carol is interested in an espresso maker for themselves as well as for entertaining. She hopes the additional cabinet and counter space she needs can be accommodated in the existing 250 square foot kitchen.

Cindy and her husband live in a condominium in a large city, but Cindy would like to remodel her kitchen to have a country look. She also wants to investigate the new solid surface materials for her countertops and would like a ventilation hood over the cooktop she is planning. Cindy must stay within the 200 square feet of kitchen space due to building limitations and hopes the coziness of a country kitchen will fit into her existing space.

I have emphasized square footage of kitchen space in this section because it is frequently the limiting factor when planning your kitchen — either due to budgetary or building limitations. Due to the wiring, plumbing, large appliances, and ex-

Name	Interest	Reference
Cathy	Work Triangle	Chapter 3 — Work Triangle
	Ovens	Chapter 5 — Ovens
Carol	Planning center	Chapter 3 — Planning Area
	Bar and drink preparation	Chapter 3 — Hospitality Area
		Chapter 7 — Sinks
		Chapter 6 — Other Cold Storage Appliances
	Espresso makers	Chapter 12 — Espresso makers
Cindy	Style of kitchen	Chapter 10 — Country kitchens
	Countertops	Chapter 9 — Solid surfaces

pensive surfaces involved, the kitchen can be the most costly room in the house. Where the average cost of a house may run from $75 to $100 per square foot, the kitchen may run $100 to $150 per square foot. Special materials and features can raise the cost per square foot even higher.

In addition to the twelve chapters referred to above, there is also an Appendix which provides brief summaries of various parts of the book, a checklist of questions under each topic to help you formulate ideas and plans for your dream kitchen, and a summary of the latest trends in kitchen building and remodeling from a survey conducted by the National Kitchen and Bath Association.

1
History of Cooking in the United States

OPEN-FIRE COOKERY

The first cooking in America was over an open fire. The native Indians roasted wild game on sticks and boiled meat and vegetables in animal skin containers over camp fires. They dropped heated stones into these skin containers to cook the food.

Cooking techniques of the Indians included roasting, broiling, boiling, and baking, but not frying. The New England Indians baked seafood surrounded by seaweed and hot coals. They also cooked dried beans by putting them in a pottery container with liquid and burying it in a pit with hot coals — the forerunner of baked beans.

The Indians prepared plant food for cooking by grinding, milling, or pounding it. They used baskets for gathering plants and seeds and then ground them with stone milling equipment, such as mortars and pestles, or manos and metates.

Food was also preserved for later use by the Indians. With the aid of a stone mortar and pestle, they were able to pulverize dried meat, suet, and berries into a mixture known as pemmican. They also preserved food by drying or burying it in caches.

These were the cooking habits of the natives encountered by the first American settlers in the early 1600s in Virginia and Massachusetts. Although the first settlers learned how to cook native foods from the Indians, they established their own kitchens and continued to use European methods of cookery.

FIREPLACE COOKERY

In the American home of the 1600s, food preparation and cooking took place in the large all-purpose room where family life centered around the fireplace. Most of these first homes contained only one room which was used for eating, sleeping, working, and cooking. The fireplace was often eight to ten feet wide so that a whole animal could be roasted in it.

All cooking was done in and over the fire in the fireplace. A large wooden pole, called a lug pole, was hung in the back of the fireplace to hold pots and kettles. However, the wooden pole did not last long since after a period of time it charred, became weak, and broke, spilling that day's meal into the fire.

During the latter part of the 1600s, iron poles were used. Yankee ingenuity made the pole into a crane, which was suspended from the side wall of the fireplace so that it could be swung out into the room to be loaded with pots and kettles. Hooks of various length, from six to fifteen inches, were used to hold the pots. A trammel, made of two pieces of iron with hooks in one and notches in the other, was used to lengthen or shorten a pot's distance from the fire.

Early cooking utensils were originally brought from the old countries, but later made by local blacksmiths. Kettles with straight sides and no covers were of many sizes and shapes. Pots, on the other hand, had bulging sides and covers and were more difficult to produce. Almost all of the cooking was done in pots and kettles. Brass and copper kettles from Europe were highly prized in the mid-1600s. They were more common in the Dutch than in the English colonies.

Pots and kettles stood on their own legs or were placed on trivets for cooking in the fireplace. The trivets were of varying heights and raised the pots above the glowing embers. The height of the trivet determined the intensity of heat and manner of cooking. The Dutch oven was a three-legged kettle with a tight-fitting cover which could be used for stews as well as baking biscuits and cornbread. When used for baking, the Dutch oven was placed in the embers and hot embers were also put on top of the cover. The Dutch oven baked in a slow manner and was used before ovens were added to fireplaces.

Long handles on implements and utensils kept the housewife as far from the fire as possible. She used several types of long handled utensils. Forks were used primarily for toasting and holding meat that was being cooked. Ladles and skimmers were used with liquids, especially soup. The ladle transferred liquids from one container to another. The pierced spoon-shaped skimmer removed floating matter from the liquid surface. Flat-sided iron turners were used to lift and turn food when frying or baking. Numerous spoons were used for stirring and tasting various types of food during their preparation.

Frying was not one of the cooking techniques of the early pioneers and did not become popular until the 1850s with the advent of the cookstove. Skillets were rare in the open hearth since spattered grease from frying was a fire hazard. The skillets that were used stood on legs over the fire and had handles up to three feet in length, so that the housewife would not burn herself when cooking. Spider skillets without long handles, but with legs, were mainly used to bake biscuits and cornbread.

Another short-legged utensil used by the early pioneers for cooking was a gridiron. This was a grid of iron bars set in a frame with short legs and a handle. It was used primarily for broiling meats, to support other cooking utensils, and to keep food warm.

Although frying and broiling were not popular forms of cookery in the early American kitchen, the roasting of tender sections of game animals and some domesticated stock was a common form of fireplace cookery. It was usually reserved for special occasions. Andirons which raised the heat by lifting the logs had special notches to support a spit on which meats were skewered. If there were no andirons for the fireplace, then the meat was put into a rope sling and suspended from the lug pole or iron crane. With either method the meat was turned occasionally and a pan was placed below the roast to catch the drippings, which were used for basting or to flavor other dishes. Later more elaborate roasting mechanisms had mechanical spits which used either human or dog power to turn them. Eventually small roasting ovens which were open to the fireside were produced.

Special utensils such as waffle irons, wafer irons, roasters, tea kettles, and swivel toasters were also used in fireplace cookery. Cake-like waffles and crisp wafers were baked between the pressed heads of waffle and wafer irons set on a grate or gridiron over hot coals. Waffle irons were usually cast with a grid pattern. Wafer irons, originally used in church services, were engraved with floral, geometric, and patriotic motifs. Special long-handled devices were used occasionally for roasting apples and chestnuts over the open fire. Bread to be toasted was placed between the bars of a swivel toaster. The toaster would be set close to the fire and rotated to toast the bread on both sides.

Although the Dutch oven was used to bake some breads in the early American kitchen, it soon became evident to the early pioneers that an oven was a necessity. The brick oven was built adjoining the fireplace and was used to bake breads, cakes, and pies, as well as such slow cooking dishes as baked beans and Indian pudding. A wood fire was built in the oven in order to heat it. After several hours, when the oven reached the desired temperature, the embers and ashes were swept from it. Breads were baked first in the very hot oven, then pies, followed by cakes and puddings. A pot of beans could bake all along, out of the way in the back of the oven.

Baking has always been a major part of American cookery. While the techniques involved in preparing baked goods have varied since the 17th century, many utensils used in baking have remained the same. At first unrefined flour and meal were hand sifted through a sieve. After the mid-19th century mechanical sifters came into common use. Dough was mixed and kneaded in round or oblong bowls often made of wood. Dough scrapers removed surplus dough from the sides of mixing bowls. Some homes had a wooden box in which dough was placed to rise. Rolling pins of wood, glass, tin, and pottery were used to flatten pastry dough.

Some baked goods required special utensils for their preparation. Round little cutters were used for cookies, biscuits and other doughs. Corrugated rollers gave cookies and other pastries a grooved surface so that they could be cut into oblong pieces after baking. Tin cookie cutters were made in numerous shapes, representing all manners of geometric, floral, animal, and human forms. Pastry jaggers (cutters) helped to seal, trim, and ornament the edges of pie crusts and cut rolled dough into various shapes.

During the 1700s, the kitchen became a separate room but retained its large fireplace and remained the center of domestic activity in the home. Cooking continued over the open fire and the kitchen was frequently the only warm room in the house in winter.

In middle class and wealthier homes in the South, kitchens were in a separate building a short distance from the house since fireplace cooking was a fire hazard. In later years, kitchens were built into the basement of the house, for coolness in the summer and warmth in the winter.

Although most fireplace cooking equipment continued to be made by the local blacksmith, cast iron pots and kettles began to be major products of American iron works around 1750. They produced both the straight-sided kettles and the pots that curved inward. The latter were more difficult to produce but were favored by the housewife because they were superior in retaining the juices and flavors of cooking food.

Pots cast between 1750 and 1830 were extremely heavy with sharp, angular ears supporting the handles. During the 1830s coke began replacing charcoal in blast furnaces. Coke furnaces operated at higher temperatures than the earlier charcoal furnaces thereby producing more delicate ironware. This resulted in smoother and more delicate pots which became lighter and more diverse in shape. By the mid-1800s large foundries utilizing mass production methods were casting pots of more uniform shapes.

Tin oven in fireplace used for roasting meat and baking.

Tin also provided an array of cooking utensils for fireplace cooking. Tin ovens for roasting and baking were valued items in the early 1800s. They were light, cheap, and easier to maneuver than the cast iron cooking utensils. Meat to be roasted in a tin oven was fastened to a spit which spanned the length of the oven. A pan underneath caught the meat drippings. Hooks on the inside of some ovens held birds or small fowl for cooking. The open side of the oven was positioned to face the fire while a door in the back allowed the cook to watch and baste the meat. The heat-reflecting tin of the oven roasted the meat on all sides.

The reflected heat of the tin was also used for baking. Cookies, cakes, breads, and pies were placed on a shelf in the oven and the heat reflected from the sides of the oven baked its contents. The biscuit roaster had a hinged door at the back so that the biscuits could be watched while they baked.

Between 1800 and 1850 the kitchen became a distinct and specialized room. Implements for food preparation and cooking became numerous and diverse. Domestic economy and receipt books were written advising the housewife on the care and management of her home. The authors of these books often discussed proper furnishings and maintenance of the kitchen, including detailed lists of kitchen utensils regarded as indispensable to efficient functioning.

A profusion of tinware was considered essential to the activities of this "modern kitchen." Although some tin household objects were manufactured in America during the 1700s, large quantities were made and used after 1800. Heavy cast iron cooking implements began to be replaced by less expensive, more efficient items of tin. Tin reflector ovens and bake ovens became common. Tin coffee roasters replaced iron skillets for roasting coffee beans. Tin was also considered a light, durable material for storage boxes and canisters.

Special utensils were developed for many kitchen tasks. There were utensils for pounding, grating, shredding, and beating food. Various forms of tin graters shredded and crushed vegetables, fruit, bread, and cheese. Graters with specialized blades shredded cabbage for sauerkraut. In the late 19th century hand-operated mechanical food choppers with revolving blades became popular, preceding Cuisinart's electric food processor by almost a century. This early food processor had two blades that turned in a tin container.

Cooking utensils of the late 1800s.

At first eggs and cake batter were beaten by hand alone, then with a slotted spoon, a fork, or a wire whisk. The first rotary egg beater was patented in 1873 by the Dover Stamping Company. These first egg beaters were wooden cylindrical shapes with either ovals of wire or two wooden blades each with a round hole. After 1870 numerous hand-operated mechanical whisks and beaters were manufactured.

Special utensils also had to be developed for herbs and spices, which were often sold in coarse form and had to be ground before they could be used. Boat-shaped herb grinders were common in the late 18th and early 19th century. Special graters were used to grind spices like nutmeg which could only be obtained whole. Sugar sold in cones was cut into suitable pieces with scissor-like nippers. Cooks used mortar and pestle to pulverize pieces of sugar, spices, and salt. Sugar and spices were stored in a variety of wooden boxes and tin containers. Salt, considered extremely valuable as a food preservative, was stored in a separate box hung near the fireplace to keep it dry.

The continuous popularity of fruits and nuts in the 1800s encouraged the introduction of numerous mechanical devices to aid in their preparation. Apple parers, for example, simplified the task of paring apples for drying and cooking. With the use of cranks, gears, belts, or springs they easily removed the skins from the apples. The earliest apple parers had wooden frames and iron blades. In the 1840s cast iron parers were introduced. Some parers also cored the apples. Apple slicers were a later innovation. Cherry stoners removed the pits from cherries. Raisin seeders worked seeds out of raisins. Hinged squeezers extracted juice from lemons. Many mechanical nutcrackers of cast iron were invented in the late 19th century to make the task of cracking nuts simpler and quicker.

As the homes grew in the late 1700s and early 1800s so did the space allotted to food preparation. Some kitchens had a buttery or small pantry where, particularly in the summer, much of the food preparation took place, including churning butter, making cheese, kneading dough, making preserves, and filling pie crusts. If the pantry was large enough, extra pots and kettles not needed for daily cooking were stored there.

IRON STOVE COOKERY

The introduction of the cast iron range and the cookstove marked a significant technological change in the kitchen. Although our forefathers claimed that food tasted better when cooked in a fireplace, the convenience of cooking on a stove far outweighed any loss of flavor.

The tremendous amount of fuel consumed in cooking over an open fireplace encouraged inventors to develop ways to concentrate heat into enclosed devices. Benjamin Franklin invented an enclosed fireplace in 1745 and in 1771 a heating stove which used bituminous coal.

In the late 1700s, another major advocate of enclosed heat devices was Benjamin Thompson, an American known as the Count of Rumford, who is credited with the invention of the cookstove. His inventions included a cylindrical oven which roasted meat more efficiently than a spit. Rumford's roaster was manufactured with limited suc-

cess by a few American companies in the early 1800s. The first American cookstove was patented in 1815. However, the fireplace continued to be used for cooking in most kitchens until the 1840s.

Based upon the idea of saving fuel by concentrating the heat source, a variety of cast iron cookstoves began to be manufactured in America during the 1830s. M.N. Stanley's innovative stove, patented in 1832, contained a boiling surface which was revolved by a hand crank allowing two of the cooking holes to receive more heat. Oval step stoves with low boiling holes and elevated ovens were to become one of the most popular cookstove types throughout the 1800s. By 1881 almost a thousand patents for cookstoves had been issued and there were more than two hundred firms manufacturing them.

When the cookstove came into common use in the late 1880s, it necessitated appropriate utensils and equipment. Cast and sheet iron kettles, pots, and pans were adapted for use with the cookstove. Iron pots and kettles, which were mass produced in iron foundries, were made smaller and lighter than before. To speed the manufacturing process and to facilitate use on the cookstove, pots were made with straighter sides and more cylindrical shapes. By the 1870s pots with recessed bottoms for setting into stove lid openings were coming into common use. Griddles, waffle irons, and coffee roasters were also often rounded on the bottom to fit on top or inside stove lid openings.

Compared with the open fireplace, a wood- or coal-burning cookstove was safer, more convenient, and more economical for food preparation. Nevertheless, considerable attention was needed to regulate the constantly changing amount of heat under the boiling lids and around the oven. The complexity of working a cookstove caused suspicion among many women concerning its reliability, even into the 1860s and 1870s.

During the 1880s, the form of many cookstoves began to change. The number of boiling lids and the size of the ovens were increased. More cookstoves used coal as a heating fuel. Gas heated

Oval cast iron cookstove with elevated oven, Ford Museum, Dearborn, MI.

Common cast iron cookstove of the late 1800s.

ranges were also introduced but were not widely used until the end of the century. Detroit became an important center of cookstove manufacturing during the late 1880s. The Detroit Stove Works purchased patterns from other cookstove manufacturers and in the 1890s became one of the largest cookstove manufacturers in the country.

Along with the new cookstoves, improved methods of preserving and storing food were available to the housewife in the late 1800s. Wooden cooling chests which held ice at the bottom had been introduced in the 1830s. Inventors realized in the 1850s that ice placed at the top of the ice-boxes preserved food more efficiently. Few successful home ice-boxes, however, were produced before the late 1800s.

The Grand Rapids Refrigerator Company pioneered many of the designs and manufacture of domestic "refrigerators." Beginning in the early 1880s the company's ice-box refrigerators were designed with ice-filled top cabinets around which cold, dry air circulated. A hardwood cabinet with picturesque carvings made the refrigerator suitable for home furnishing at the time. Refrigerators, however, were primarily used in city homes for storing milk, butter, and other perishable food in the summer. Farm homes used their well or spring house for cold storage.

Although the refrigerator was a means of storing fresh food, other methods of food preservation were also practiced in the home. The early American families butchered, cured, and smoked their meats. They dried fruits, particularly apples, for later use and made jams and jellies. Fruits and vegetables were cooked and stored in crocks or ceramic jars in root cellars.

In 1809, Nicholas Appert found that food could be preserved for long periods of time in hermetically sealed glass containers that had been sterilized with heat. Preserving fruits, vegetables, jams, and meat in this manner became common for home use after 1858 when John Mason patented a thread screw type glass jar. Many later manufacturers of similar jars utilized Mason's name with their own products. Ceramic jars used since colonial times to preserve food were manufactured in great quantities in the late 19th century. Tin preserving containers also became common during that time. Wide funnels of tin or pottery were often used to fill preserving jars. Large kettles were manufactured for boiling the canned goods.

Tin storage containers were also quite popular during the late 1800s, although canned and packaged foods were becoming more common. These containers were light, durable, and attractive for home or store use. Some elaborate canisters contained numerous condiments and staples within a complex series of compartments.

THE VICTORIAN KITCHEN

By the late 1800s the kitchen had become a distinct entity. No longer was it the all-purpose room for family activities centered around a fireplace which was also used for cooking. The Victorian kitchen was a bright, cheerful, cozy room with a cookstove, sink, and in many homes also an icebox. The walls of the kitchen were painted and the floor was usually covered with linoleum since that was easier to care for than a wood floor.

The kitchen sink was made of iron, soapstone, or crockery, but since most kitchens did not have indoor plumbing, water had to be brought in buckets from the outside. The cookstove burned coal, wood, or corncobs. It cooked and baked the food and also provided warmth in the winter. Near the stove was a reservoir of water, just in case there was a fire. The kitchen table was made of wood and most of the food preparation was done on it.

With new utensils, gadgets, and "modern" conveniences, the housewife had some leisure time. A comfortable chair was added to the kitchen so that she could sit and do some sewing or mending while the bread or pies were baking.

Most Victorian kitchens had an attached pantry where non-perishable foods and cooking ingredients were stored, as well as pottery mixing bowls, crocks for pickling, baking sheets, and large pots and pans. Farm homes also had butter churns and molds, and cheese making equipment stored in the pantry.

THE 20TH CENTURY KITCHEN

The 20th century kitchen became increasingly more efficient and standardized. Its arrangement of furnishings reflected greater awareness of the need for convenience, orderliness, and hygiene. Wooden work tables were often covered with oil cloth, linoleum, or enamelled metal for cleanliness and neatness.

Kitchen storage cabinets and cupboards at the beginning of the century, although free standing at first, facilitated the organization of the task of preparing food. Many free standing kitchen cabinets had a built-in flour bin with a sifter. Potatoes and root vegetables were stored in the bottom of the cabinet.

The beginning of the 1900s was the age of kitchen gadgetry and labor saving devices, not to be outdone until our present time. There were graters and grinders, from the tiny nutmeg grater to iron sausage grinders. Potato ricers and graters were used not only for potatoes, but also to grate horseradish, and to make relishes and baby food. During butchering season the iron sausage stuffer was in almost constant use. Apple peelers and cherry stoners were a necessity in almost every household. Stove lid lifters and ice tongs, along with a long iron poker for the kitchen stove, were used in every kitchen.

Students of scientific housekeeping suggested ways to improve the kitchen work space before World War I, but manufacturers disregarded the studies and continued to design incompatible equipment until about the mid-1930s. After that

A twentieth century dream kitchen. From the Adaptable House, Portland, Oregon. Photo courtesy of Wilsonart.

time, the term "streamlining" was applied lavishly to kitchen design. Continuous countertop work surfaces and built-in cabinets were combined with standardized gas and electrical systems and plumbing to form efficient integrated work units. The rounded corners and smooth continuous work surfaces facilitated cleaning in the stream-lined kitchen. The 1936 Electro-Chef Range had the up-to-date features of countertop, storage spaces, and temperature regulation. Its legs, which were shaped like Duncan Phyfe table legs, raised the cooking unit off the floor for easy cleaning.

The electric range, developed between 1890 and 1910, took its form from the gas range. It was often topped with enamelled porcelain and was constructed to the same height as the other working surfaces in the kitchen. By the mid-1930s, the electric range had been greatly improved and was competing with the gas range for popularity.

Electricity began to replace ice, kerosene, and gas as the major cooling agent for refrigerators. By the 1930s, electric refrigerators with thermostatic controls and porcelain interiors became the standard element in most kitchens. Dishwashers, which were introduced about 1910, also became electrically powered by the 1930s.

Small electric appliances such as toasters and waffle irons became widely accepted during the 1920s and 1930s. These light, portable devices easily lent themselves to the increasing standardization of the kitchen. Aluminum was considered the best material for cookware during this time, although tin, cast iron, and copper were also popular.

At the 1939 World's Fair, the kitchen was one of the few rooms in the home where the entire space was being modernized. By the late 1940s, streamlined kitchens were typical, with built-in storage cabinets and continuous counter work surfaces. The all-white enamelled electric range with an automatically regulated timer and temperature control became an established component of the streamlined kitchen.

After the second World War, as the women entered the work force, they wanted more efficiency in their kitchens. In the 1950s, Cornell University initiated a series of studies to determine the most efficient use of kitchens. The result of these studies was the triangle concept which was based on three distinct work areas in the kitchen — storage and preparation, cooking, and cleanup. The study also recommended ideal distances between these work stations.

In the late 1950s, as a result of technologies developed during World War II, new materials, smaller motors, and other technology innovations became a part of the modern kitchen. Aluminum began to be used for cookware, laminates for countertops, and small powerful motors made possible the development of hand-held electrical appliances.

Although microwave energy for cooking was discovered in the early 1940s as a fringe benefit of radar research, it was not until the 1970s that the microwave oven was developed and perfected for home use. It reduced cooking time of most foods by 50 to 75 percent. The computer age of the '80s revolutionized control panels on major appliances. Further development of small cooking devices has enabled the busy working women to prepare meals quickly.

After some years of streamlined and clinical looking kitchens, the working woman decided that she wanted a more relaxing, friendly, and efficient kitchen. Since many women are away from home during the day, they want the kitchen to be a place where the family can share in each others' activities while dinner is being prepared.

Once again the kitchen is the place to be. To use an overworked expression it is again "the heart of the home." It is no longer the place where Mom works alone, but a place where all comers are welcome, where the family gathers, and where guests pitch in and help with the meal.

In the past few decades we have also relearned what our ancestors appreciated — that family activities are more relaxed when they take place in an informal setting near the area associated with food, companionship, and love. In colonial days it was the hearth; today it is the kitchen.

2
The Basic Use of the Kitchen

The typical kitchen design incorporates at least three basic mealtime activities — preparing the food, serving it, and cleaning up. Many kitchens have space and facilities for eating breakfast and lunch, and even dinner. Also many of today's kitchens have become an adjunct to the living area and in fact, the kitchen is frequently the focal point of family life.

To me, the word "kitchen" evokes memories of my grandmother, who was a caterer in Europe, baking her wonderful pastries. As a child, I would watch her prepare beautiful entrées and would peek out through the kitchen door as they were being served to her guests in the dining room. Later, after coming to America when I was in my early teens, I remember my mother and I spending many hours in the kitchen learning to cook in the "American style" — making pies, fried chicken, and baked beans, along with her German specialities. Throughout my married life I have had various kitchens ranging from a tiny one in a university student housing project to my present spacious "dream kitchen."

Before World War II many families could afford to hire a cook, so the family spent little time in the kitchen — perhaps only to steal something from the ice-box or refrigerator. Following the War, most of my friends became the family cook. They adopted the practice of letting the children play in the kitchen while they cooked. As the years passed, the kitchen became a place for the family and close friends to gather and discuss the events of the day. Having neighbors or friends drop by for a cup of coffee in the kitchen became a delightful daily occurrence. We quickly found out, without thinking about it, that the kitchen is inherently a cheerful and hospitable place that encourages relaxed and friendly social exchange.

Many of us in the '50s and '60s took on two careers — that of the working woman and the homemaker-cook. It was this dual career that prompted us to want more efficient kitchens. We wanted cabinets that were easy to keep clean, refrigerators that did not need defrosting, self cleaning ovens, and cooktops where spills would vanish with the wipe of a sponge or cloth. The manufacturers of kitchen cabinets, floors, and appliances responded to our needs and helped us create kitchens which became efficient and pleasurable places to prepare our family's meals.

We have also brought other household activities into the kitchen and participate in them while cooking. Many kitchens have a television set so that the cook can watch the Oprah Winfrey show while preparing a meal. The barbecue in or near the kitchen has become an additional cooking facility. The wet bar is a common feature in a corner of the kitchen or the nearby family room. Also fairly common today is a desk in the kitchen for meal planning, making shopping lists, talking on the telephone, and even bill-paying. Kitchens are adjacent to or a part of family rooms so that the cook can participate in family activities while she is working in the kitchen.

Since kitchen activities involve the entire family, kitchen planning and design cannot be left entirely to architects and builders with only intermittent input from the family. Ideally the kitchen should be designed by the family cook with comments and suggestions from the rest of the family, in addition to the architect, builder, or professional kitchen planner. The latter has been trained to design and organize kitchens, to develop functional floor plans, and to help you select appliances and cabinets to suit your lifestyle. Many of these kitchen planners are members of the National Kitchen and Bath Association. Fortunately, there are also excellent books on the market and in libraries that teach the fundamentals of kitchen design to help the family realize their dream kitchen.

The kitchen is a very personal room primarily devoted to the activities of the family cook and thus should reflect his or her preferences. In many modern families, however, this is complicated by the presence of more than one cook. The children make their own snacks or meals, the father makes salads or bread and does the barbecuing, while the older daughter likes to experiment with baking, entrées, and desserts on occasion. That is why kitchen planning and design should be a shared family experience.

While few of us have the luxury of designing our own complete kitchen that does not mean that we cannot dream about it. Besides, kitchens can be remodeled and modernized within existing structures. Even a small apartment kitchen can be redesigned to better fit our individual lifestyle.

For example, a small apartment provides only minimum counter and storage space. Even the appliances have to be scaled down to fit. Yet this space can be configured to provide a special place for food preparation, baking, drink preparation, and even informal dining.

A family with active teenagers needs a kitchen with additional kitchen equipment. A recent survey found that most teenagers know how to use a microwave oven and can cook by time if not by instructions. However, there are many children of working parents who start dinner preparations after school and are well versed in the use of cooking equipment. My neighbor's teenage daughter of fourteen even went so far recently as to prepare a very exotic Russian dinner for the family.

Preparing meals for a family with several children requires a kitchen with such facilities as a microwave oven for quick meal preparation, toaster ovens for small meals, and immersion blenders for milk shakes and other drinks. With today's busy lifestyles, we find family members wanting to eat at different times and different types of food. This can require separate and even duplicate facilities.

With all of these various cooking activities, a well-designed kitchen can bring a family closer together during the hours they are home. As every mother knows, a play area in or just adjacent to the kitchen is a necessity when the children are very small. As they get older, the kitchen becomes a place for do-it-yourself cooking and family discussions. My husband often likes to chat with me while I am cooking dinner and while he is watching the evening news and reading the paper. Therefore we have designed our kitchen so that the breakfast nook is open to the work area.

However, there are many cooks who do not want all of this family activity in the kitchen. They also do not want their guests in the kitchen where they would see the cook working and possibly feel obligated to help. I, too, prefer peace and quiet in the kitchen, particularly when I am experimenting with a new recipe. Therefore, I prefer to keep my kitchen work area out of the normal family traffic flow while still keeping the room open to the informal eating and living area.

Your dream kitchen should also reflect your lifestyle. If you enjoy cooking and eating outdoors, your kitchen should have easy access to that area. If you like to listen to the radio or watch television while cooking, then there should be a convenient place to put them. If you cook with fresh herbs and like to grow them indoors then there should be a place with natural lighting to do so.

Regardless of the size or type of kitchen, its basic use is the same — the preparation of food. However, each of us must decide which type of kitchen is best suited to our needs, which makes meal preparation more enjoyable, and which uses the space most efficiently.

THE COOK'S KITCHEN

Almost all modern kitchens include as standard equipment a sink; a cooktop and built-in oven or a stand-alone range; and a refrigerator-freezer combination. The cooking unit has a ventilation system to get rid of unwanted cooking odors. Today, most kitchens also include a microwave oven, a dishwasher, and a garbage disposal.

Additional features depend on the needs of the individual cook. For example, the cook who makes fancy pastries, her own pasta, and does a great deal of entertaining needs more work and storage space than the cook who prepares simple meals. The latter, however, may require stir-frying, barbecuing, and other quick meal-preparation facilities such as a microwave oven.

Regardless of what type of cooking you do, there are certain basic design principles that can make your dream kitchen a comfortable place in which to work. To me one of the most important aspects of a comfortable and well-designed kitchen is that the countertops are a comfortable height. Since I am short, I like my countertops at 34½ to 35 inches in height. A tall person such as Julia Child, who is 5 feet, 10 inches tall, would probably like them at 38 inches. The normal countertop height is 36 inches. Real estate agents will point out, however, that if you are planning your kitchen with later resale of the house in mind, it is best to conform to the normal height.

The cook's dream kitchen should also have flooring that is comfortable to stand on for long periods of time. Just because a floor looks pretty, does not mean it is going to be comfortable. For my dream kitchen, I chose a beautiful ceramic tile floor that simulated old stones and have found that the slight surface variations are hard on the feet and legs over long periods of time.

In planning your dream kitchen, remember that you can never have too much storage space. In a large new kitchen, you may think you have too much storage space, but it fills up quickly. I have a weakness for pottery and ceramic cooking and serving pieces and find that casseroles with domed lids and fancy top handles are awkward to store. My other weakness is the latest in electrical appliances, so I am always trying to find additional storage space in my kitchen. I agree with the person who said, if you have not used something in two years, get rid of it.

Space can quickly limit the number, size, and style of the equipment you use in cooking. I have found that it is usually a problem in the average kitchen to find storage space for small electrical appliances, cooking and baking utensils, large amounts of essential ingredients (pantry), china, and glassware. The problem of storing baking sheets can be solved if you store them in a cabinet with vertical partitions. Molds and baking pans are difficult to store since they usually do not fit inside of each other and do not stack neatly.

Regardless of whether your dream kitchen is large or small, there are some basic decisions you can make to achieve more efficiency. First of all, determine what appliances you need for maximum efficiency. If your permanent fixtures, major appliances, sink, and cabinets, do not meet your needs think about changing them. Discard any small appliances, cookware, and gadgets you do not use. However, there are trade-offs. You might choose a smaller sink to gain more counter space; combine a microwave and convection oven in one unit; install a small additional sink for the other cook in your family to alleviate a traffic problem; or do structural changes such as closing an infrequently used doorway in the kitchen to gain additional cabinet space.

If your dream kitchen is small, Organization (with a capital O) is the key to efficiency. Not too long ago, we rented an apartment for several months while our house was being built. With a very small kitchen, I was forced to alter my methods of food preparation. Due to limited space, it

Multiple storage space is provided in this U-shaped kitchen. Skylight provides extra daytime illumination. Cabinets in oak style New Hampton by Quaker Maid. Photo courtesy of Quaker Maid.

Center island in kitchen with sufficient space for traffic can serve as a buffet table. Amherst Kitchen by Quaker Maid. Photo courtesy of Quaker Maid.

was necessary to clean up after each preparation and cooking task. I also found that smaller versions of electrical appliances were better suited to a small kitchen.

Many working couples prefer a small kitchen because meals are prepared quickly and cleanup is at a minimum and they only do more extensive cooking projects on the weekends. Sad to say, however, many small kitchens are not designed with even this small amount of cooking in mind. They only provide the bare necessities of cooking, refrigeration, and cleanup, with very little counter or storage space, and what little there is, is frequently in the wrong place.

Many European manufacturers, such as Gaggenau, Miele, AEG, and Creda, as well as America's General Electric and White-Westinghouse have begun offering appliances designed with the small kitchen in mind. For example, they are producing small wall ovens ranging from 21 to 24 inches in width, instead of the normal 24 to 30 inches. These same manufacturers also have reduced-size cooktops, refrigerators, and dishwashers. Most of the major appliance manufacturers make 24-inch deep refrigerator/freezers which fit flush with standard cabinets and do not jut out into the room. Some also produce 20-inch deep ranges, microwaves that fit under the cabinets, 18-inch wide dishwashers, and even dishwashers that fit under a shallow sink.

A KITCHEN FOR TWO COOKS

Even in a small kitchen, two gourmet cooks can work side by side by installing two separate two- or three-burner electric cooktops. Small triple sinks are also available for this type of kitchen, and to maximize storage space in minimal square footage, cabinets with pull-out shelving and lazy Susans can be custom-designed. For added storage space, cabinets should reach the ceiling with the top shelves allotted to infrequently used items.

Larger kitchens with various counter and appliance configurations can easily accommodate two cooks. If they both share in meal preparation you might want to provide room for two sinks, as well as two separate cooktops. I recently saw a very attractive two-cook kitchen with an octagonal center island that had two cooktops separated by one leg of the octagon. Three of the other parts of the tiled octagon opposite the cooktops were used for informal dining. An attractive copper hood for ventilation completed this focal point in the two-cook kitchen.

If there are two cooks in your dream kitchen there should be enough space for comfortable traffic flow. You do not want to bump into each other while one is transporting a hot and heavy pot of pasta to the sink to be drained. For easy passage, the aisles should be at least 4½ feet wide. This provides enough room for one cook to walk behind the other without disturbing him or her.

In a larger kitchen used by two cooks, there should be definite work areas for each. With two cooks in a family, each usually specializes in some aspect of meal preparation. Many men like to prepare the meats and do the baking. One of our friends makes all of the desserts while his wife prepares the rest of the meal. In another case, the husband prepares the entrée and the wife does the salad or soup and the dessert. Whatever the arrangement, separate and suitable work space is needed if peace is to be kept in the family.

Regardless of whether your dream kitchen is for one or two cooks, it is advisable to have a specific counter area for food preparation with food processor, mixing bowls, casseroles, canned goods, and spices stored in cabinets underneath, overhead, or nearby. It is also convenient to have a separate baking center where a portable or stand-alone mixer, mixing bowls, baking sheets, baking pans, flour and sugar canisters, and other baking ingredients can be stored. I also like to have enough space for a cookbook stand on the counter, although I frequently photocopy the recipe and paste it to the refrigerator door with magnets. A small copy machine has become a "must" in my household.

When I entertain, I like to serve the main

Large kitchen with double sink, bar sink, and spacious countertops can easily accommodate two cooks. Hampton V cabinets by Quaker Maid. Photo courtesy of Quaker Maid.

course on individual plates from the kitchen. My 4 × 8 foot center island is ideal for this type of food service because I can spread out six to eight plates in succession. Since the cooktop is also located on one side of the island it is easy get hot food to the waiting plates. I have also found that the island, which has a ceramic tile top, serves as an attractive buffet table for guests. Most islands have sufficient space around them to accommodate the flow of traffic comfortably.

Gas or electric cooktops are a matter of personal preferences, although some cooks want both. A gas commercial-type range, if space permits, has become a popular item in many so-called "gourmet" kitchens.

A large refrigerator and freezer are a necessity for those who do a great amount of entertaining or have a large family. Two separate units should also be considered. Not having space for separate units, I solved the problem by installing an extra refrigerator and a stand-up freezer in the basement. Often you can find good buys on new appliances at your dealer's "dent and scratch sale" for use as secondary food storage.

The cook's kitchen should have a sink large enough to accommodate a number of pots and pans soaking at the same time. The choice of a single, double, or even triple sink is up to you. I have had both single and double sinks and presently have a very large deep sink with a small side sink (which I rarely use).

If you have the space you may want two full-size sinks, one near the preparation area and the other nearer the eating area or dining room. Or you might choose to have one large sink and a smaller one in a central island. Also two dishwashers and two disposals are very helpful if you entertain a lot. Every time I have a large dinner party I am sorry that I did not put in a second dishwasher. One avid cook I know has installed her second dishwasher in a walk-through pantry connecting the kitchen and dining room.

The number and choice of small electrical appliances in the kitchen is up to each cook, depending on his or her cooking style. For example, some cooks like to use an electric griddle to make pancakes, others prefer a griddle on top of an electric or gas burner, and still others use the griddle attachment of their cooktop. I prefer to use a griddle on top of the burner because it is easier to clean and store, although I do use the griddle module of my cooktop when I am cooking for more people.

Last, but by no means least, is the need for ample storage space. I find that there can never be enough of it. In the cook's dream kitchen there should be storage space for pantry goods; cooking, mixing, and baking utensils; dishes; glassware; cooking gadgets; and a shelf or two for cookbooks.

A separate butler's pantry can be a passageway between the kitchen and dining room, or space permitting, be tucked into an alcove. The butler's pantry area can include a bar sink and an under-counter refrigerator, making this an ideal space for serving drinks and preparing hors d'oeuvres. A second dishwasher could also be installed.

THE EAT-IN KITCHEN

With today's informal lifestyles, there are no rules about where you eat. Since many kitchens are now showplaces in themselves, eating in the kitchen has become an accepted practice, even with guests. The eating area can be a counter, a breakfast nook, or an old-fashioned kitchen table at one end of the room. Whatever the style, it should be comfortable – a friendly place for eating and social exchange. Natural light from windows and proper artificial lighting can enhance the eating area and the enjoyment of food.

Each family's dining space needs are different. A retired couple may only need a small breakfast nook, while growing families want space for eating and for children's homework and play. Others may want to use the kitchen for informal entertaining.

Regardless of where the dining space is located make sure that the table or counter will accommodate the number of people who usually use the area. If you entertain informally in the kitchen,

The eating area in this country kitchen by Quaker Maid serves family and guests. Photo courtesy of Quaker Maid.

plan the eating area so that it can be expanded to accommodate guests. We use an expandable round table, which with an extra leaf can seat six comfortably.

The dining area can be an integral part of the kitchen work area or it can be a separate entity. In addition to dining, this eating area can be used to relax during the day with a cup of coffee or for meal planning in lieu of a desk area. How relaxed this area is depends on the plan of the kitchen, whether it is one large room or is separated by a peninsula, cabinets, or other dividers.

The farmhouse kitchen of years ago was an open one with a large table in the center. Farm wives enjoyed neighbors and friends dropping in to exchange news and recipes. Today a large table in the center of the kitchen is still in style if space is available. Lacking the space, some of the concept can be retained by designing the center island with an eating space. This is convenient for the busy cook and provides space for quick snacks and impromptu lunches. Many such islands are designed to include a cooktop and grill at one end and a stepped-down eating area at the other. A similar dining arrangement can also be located on the back of a peninsula separating the kitchen from a living area.

In keeping with most of today's kitchen designs, informal eating areas are often located at one end of the kitchen and may be along one wall, in a corner, or in a bay window. Very small kitchens can have some eating area, even if it is a fold-down table or small counter. Wood-Mode makes a 32-inch wide pullout table that lets you dine in the kitchen when there is no room for a standard table. The pullout table extends to 54 inches and disappears into its own cabinet when not in use. It is available in a variety of woods, laminates, styles, and finishes. Another option for a small dining area, if there are only two in the family, is an ice cream parlor table for two.

On the other hand, a banquette (booth), either semicircular or with one or two benches makes a cozy eating area for a larger family. This type of eating arrangement is also a space saver, since it takes up less room than a free-standing table and chairs. However, banquettes are not practical for a family with small children who will tend to climb over each other to get away from the table. If you are using a free-standing table for eating, it does not have to be centered in the dining area. Sometimes off-center placement may improve traffic patterns and gain floor space.

The dining area should be in a part of the kitchen that is away from the sink, so that dirty dishes and pots and pans are not visible to the diners. I prefer a dining area with some type of division, such as a peninsula, and particularly appreciate the room division when I have prepared a meal in a hurry and left a mess in the kitchen.

Most people like light and a view while they are eating. Whatever the eating space, it is nice to have something to look at other than the wall. If possible, place your eating area on an exterior wall where there are either windows or a space where they may be added. Our 10 × 11 foot breakfast nook has an 8-foot sliding door on one wall which gives us a view of the woods behind the house. A side wall, which separates the breakfast nook from the family room, is actually a parapet with spindles that provides both isolation and a feeling of openness.

There is an almost infinite variety of eating arrangements that can be adapted to meet special situations. In our apartment we used a small 36-inch dropleaf table to create a separate breakfast area. Being only 5 feet tall, I rejected the use of high counters and stools when we built our house because I found them awkward to use. However, a friend has the best of both worlds. The peninsula dividing her kitchen from the eating area has just enough room for two counter stools. Her young children eat at the counter while she uses the other side for food preparation and the adults eat at the table beyond the peninsula.

For those who enjoy eating at a counter there should be a minimum of 22 inches of width and at least 18 inches of depth for each eating space to accommodate place settings and glasses. Also, about 14 inches of overhang is necessary to provide knee space under the counter. A general rule of thumb is that the seat of the stool should be 12 inches lower than the counter height, thus a 24-inch stool is needed for a 36-inch high counter. If this eating space is within the flow of traffic, there should be sufficient room for someone to pass — at least 3½ feet between the counter and the wall or the next obstruction.. When not in use stools can be slid under the counter.

An eating area can take up quite a bit of floor space. Most kitchen designers feel that 64 square feet (an 8 × 8 foot area) is the minimum for a breakfast nook which accommodates four people. A round pedestal table looks more spacious and can accommodate several more diners comfortably than can a four-legged table of a similar size. A 44-inch round table will seat six, but a minimum of 36 inches should be added to allow chairs to be pulled out and people to pass behind the chairs when they are occupied. Thus, a three-walled dining alcove with a 44-inch round table requires a minimum room size of 10 feet by 10 feet.

A glass-topped table for dining, whether round, square or oblong will make any space look larger. Being able to see through the table makes it almost disappear and gives the area a spacious effect. I love them, but they are a pain in the neck to keep clean, especially if you have young children who are messy eaters.

Regardless of what style of informal dining you choose, there should be a service center near your eating area. A toaster and coffee maker should be stored near the area where breakfast is served. An appliance garage near the table on a counter keeps these appliances handy, but out of the way when not in use.

Also near the dining area of your dream kitchen you will want to include storage space for the table linens, china, glassware, and cutlery which you use every day. Salt and pepper shakers, favorite seasonings, relishes and condiments, breakfast cereals, and vitamins or other medication taken on a regular basis should also be stored near the eating area.

Adequate lighting is another important feature in the dining area since it will not only be used for eating, but for reading, homework, and even games. It must be bright enough to see the food, but also dim enough at times for a more social evening. We have installed dimmer switches to give us the intensity of light we desire. If there is not adequate daylight in your eating area, a skylight could be installed if structurally feasible.

Natural light for the dining area can come from windows, sliding glass doors, or a skylight. The dining table can be placed in an alcove with circular windows, or under a domed skylight.

THE "KEEPING ROOM" KITCHEN

Today much of our time is spend outside of the home. With the two wage-earner family and children in school, there is an increased emphasis on spending more of our time when we are at home interacting with one another. Sociologists and home planners say that the kitchen of the '90s will be a large, multi-purpose room, as it was in the 1700s and 1800s.

This multi-purpose room — often called a "keeping room" — is divided into separate living, eating, and cooking areas to meet the needs of the entire family. It is equipped with television, computer, music center, comfortable lounging furniture, and a dining set in addition to the normal kitchen items. Although the "keeping room" has an open feeling, it does not have to be an enormously large area, only large enough to be comfortable and have sufficient space for family and cooking activities.

This type of room can also be a large country kitchen that includes a dining and a seating area, the latter two being divided from the kitchen by a peninsula. A sink or cooktop can be placed in the peninsula so that you can easily participate in the family activities while cooking. In lieu of a peninsula, a counter-height piece of furniture can be placed strategically to divide the kitchen from the living area. This piece of furniture can also be used for buffet service.

The cozy atmosphere of a keeping room type of kitchen with a fire in the fireplace during the winter is very popular in the colder parts of the country and is reminiscent of the heritage of those areas, particularly New England and the Midwest. The kitchen area of these country kitchens sometimes includes an old-fashioned wood- or coal-burning range, which is used for cooking as well as heating during the winter.

The decor of the entire room, kitchen and family-living area, should be the same. However, the kitchen floor can be different from that of the living area, for example one tiled and the other carpeted. Usually these keeping or country kitchens have traditional decor of the area in which the home is located, such as early American in New England, a farmhouse theme in the Midwest, or Spanish decor in the Southwest.

3
Working in Your Kitchen

THE WORK TRIANGLE

With today's varied styles of cooking, such as microwaving, stir-frying, cooking with a crockpot, and barbecuing, many of the design concepts of the standard kitchen triangle — the foundation of kitchen design — are no longer applicable. This work triangle, developed by Cornell University in the 1950s, defined the basic kitchen activities — cooking, preparation, and cleanup — and their inter-relationship within the kitchen. More specifically it defined the inter-relationships between the stove, the refrigerator, and the sink.

The Cornell University concept of the kitchen work triangle created more efficient kitchens at the time. The work triangle tried to limit the number of steps necessary to prepare a meal. The concept is still the basis of kitchen planning, although today we also focus on other activity centers, some of which are included in the basic work triangle.

According to the Cornell University study, the kitchen is composed of three work centers or areas — preparation, cooking, and cleanup. Each area includes either a major appliance or a sink, and counter and storage space around them. The study also gave suggested distances between these areas for optimum efficiency.

The traditional work triangle encompasses a total distance of not less than 12 feet and not more than 22 feet. The recommended distance between the sink and refrigerator is 4 to 7 feet, the sink to the range 4 to 6 feet, and the range to the refrigerator 4 to 9 feet. Normal work patterns are from the refrigerator to the sink to the range in a counterclock-wise motion. In most kitchen plans this triangle is still applicable.

TODAY'S KITCHEN CONCEPT

Today, we think in terms of more than three areas depending on the number and type of appliances that are required. However, many kitchen designers still adhere to the traditional theory of the work triangle and it is a good starting point for kitchen planning.

The original work triangle was based on the stand-alone stove which combined the cooktop and ovens. Modern design has separated the cooktop and ovens and made them built-ins. In most kitchens the wall ovens are installed away from the cooktop, creating another cooking area. Built-in indoor barbecues, a second cooktop, built-in or free-standing microwave ovens, a bar, a second preparation area with an additional sink, and numerous small electrical cooking appliances have created a number of diversified cooking areas.

The preparation area, which traditionally centered around the refrigerator and a nearby pantry, has also changed. Today it is not centered around the refrigerator but is defined as the area where you spend most of your time in food preparation. With this activity, many cooks have separate areas for chopping vegetables, baking, preparing sandwiches, and making salads.

The only leg of the work triangle remaining basically intact is the cleanup area, which is centered around the sink. However, this area has become more complex since the original work triangle concept was developed. The cleanup center now includes a garbage disposal, a dishwasher, and more recently a trash compactor has been added.

Other work areas in today's kitchens include a separate area for the refrigerator/freezer with an adjacent countertop; a serving area, which is close to the eating area; a baking area; a menu planning area; and a hospitality area where drinks and hors d'oeuvres are prepared.

If there is more than one cook in the kitchen or if your kitchen accommodates a lot of friends who like to cook together, the traditional triangle scheme of sink, stove, and refrigerator does not work too well because it hinders traffic flow. The general traffic flow in the kitchen should be outside of the triangle so that meal preparation and cleanup can be done without interruption.

The ideal kitchen should have adequate space in which to move around, but should not be so large that you take a hike every time you need a tool, a utensil, or an ingredient. It has been recommended that a comfortable kitchen encompass 100 square feet and not be larger than 150 square feet. I think that size depends on individual cooking styles and needs. I love my 300 square foot kitchen which is 15 feet by 20 feet with an island in the center.

In a small kitchen where there are usually no wasted steps, the distances between the work triangle and storage near the work areas is not critical. In a small area, it is a good idea to keep the appliances and cabinets that have the widest doors in one area and make the aisles in front of them wider. If there is not enough room for standard 24-inch cabinets on two walls, use more shallow units on one wall which will still give you some work space and good storage.

There is one rule that should be followed regardless of your kitchen plan: Keep the supplies and utensils you need for a particular task as close as possible and assemble the ingredients and utensils before you begin to cook.

THE PREPARATION AREA

The traditional preparation area of the work triangle included the refrigerator, storage cabinets, and counter space. Today that term means the area where you prepare food. Over the years we have modified the preparation area to include several work surfaces, for mixing, chopping, slicing, baking, or salad making. Most cooks, including me, prefer that this area be located between the refrigerator and sink so that fruits and vegetables can be taken out of the refrigerator, washed, and prepared within the space of a few steps.

Since we now have a great variety of movable electrical appliances to aid in food preparation, we no longer have to limit ourselves to using them in a designated area. Battery-driven, cordless mixers, blenders, and choppers can go anywhere in the kitchen — the preparation areas or the cooking areas. They can be stored beneath the preparation counter or near the cooktop since they are used in both places.

The heavier small appliances are usually located and used in a permanent area, which becomes the major preparation center. Most people store these appliances, such as the often-used food processor, on the open counter or in an appliance garage.

The appliance garage is an enclosed space between the upper cabinets and the countertop with either swing-open doors or a tambour (roll-up) door. In my preparation area, I found that the appliance garage took up too much valuable counter space, so I opted to store my small appliances on roll out shelves in the base cabinet beneath the main preparation area. I do have a can opener on top of the counter since I found it was too inefficient to keep it in a cabinet.

In addition to appliance storage, the preparation center should include storage space for mixing bowls, measuring cups and spoons, and gadgets such as a potato peeler, and lemon zester. Also leave a space for a knife rack to hold your favorite cutting and chopping implements close at hand.

Small electrical appliances such as a hand mixer, immersion blender, and juicer are also stored in the preparation area. Spices used in food preparation should be stored in two places — where the food is prepared and where it is cooked. You will want to keep duplicates of the most-often used spices near the cooktop.

My main preparation area is the counter between the refrigerator and the sink, although I also often use the short end of the island opposite the refrigerator. I like to work at the island since that space is larger than the counter area, particularly if I have to assemble many different ingredients and use a variety of utensils.

In many kitchens the preparation center is also the baking center. However, in kitchens where there is sufficient room, particularly those with peninsulas and islands, the baking center is not confined to the same area as food preparation.

Many cooks have a built-in chopping block in their food preparation center. I had this in one kitchen and took it out because I felt that the built-in chopping block could never be thoroughly cleaned. To me a wooden chopping block retains food odors, and I much prefer the small acrylic ones that can be taken to the sink and scrubbed.

There are many mobile islands (butcher blocks) on the market which can be used for preparation or baking centers. Their top surface is either hardwood or laminated. Being mobile, the unit can be moved as a work surface anywhere in the room or even set up for a buffet service. If you prefer this approach, be sure to have sufficient room in the kitchen for this mobile unit.

The preparation center is often the home for the microwave oven. By locating the microwave oven in the same area you will be able to save unnecessary steps. I built my microwave oven into the cabinets above the preparation center because a great deal of microwave cookery involves step-by-step preparation, removing the dish from the oven, stirring or adding something to it, and then replacing it in the microwave oven for further cooking. Defrosting and heating ingredients, which can be part of the preparation process, is another function of the microwave unit.

THE COOKING AREA

The cooking area in the past was centered around a single appliance — the range, which included surface burners and one or two ovens. One of the best cooking units I ever had was a 1972 General Electric stand-alone oven with four burners, a work surface, and two ovens, one large and the other small. The small 14-inch oven was ideal for pies, a loaf of bread, and small casseroles, while the large one could handle a 22 pound turkey.

Today the cooking area can still encompass a stand-alone or drop-in range, but it usually centers around a built-in cooktop, with or without modular units. The cooking area should be well ventilated with either an overhead or downdraft system to remove unwanted odors, grease particles, and steam. There are a number of such self-contained units on the market today.

Another cooking area is created by wall ovens, which are used for baking, roasting, and broiling. Large barbecues often built into a bricked area of the kitchen not only present a beautiful atmosphere, but an additional cooking area.

With the use of multiple small appliances, the cooking center has expanded to include a stand-alone microwave oven, a toaster oven, an electric frying pan, a crockpot, a griddle, an electric wok, and a deep fat fryer. These actually can be used anywhere in the kitchen near an electric outlet, but are usually placed near the ventilation system which is over or built into the cooktop.

I have two ventilation systems in my kitchen. One is a downdraft with my General Electric cooktop and the other is built into my General Electric microwave oven which is mounted over the preparation area. I use the latter for all of my wok stir-frying so that the overhead fan can pull the odors out. In this way I can still use the cooktop for other cooking activities.

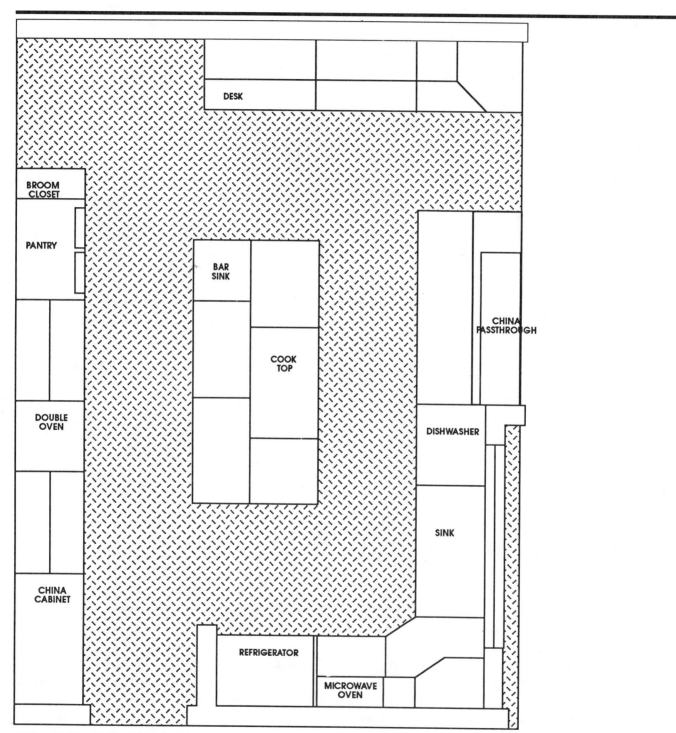

Hilde and Allan Lee's kitchen.

If you are using a built-in cooktop with the ovens adjacent to it, provide at least 18 inches of counter space between the cooktop and the ovens so that there will be enough room to put a hot casserole or roaster pan. Even if the cooktop is not located adjacent to the ovens there should 18 inches of counter space adjacent to the wall ovens to accommodate hot pans coming out of the oven. If that is not feasible then there should be counter space within 48 inches of the front of the appliance. Many ovens are located away from the cooktop because with today's cooking habits ovens are not used as frequently as microwave ovens, toaster ovens, and cooktops.

Although there is counter space on each side of my wall ovens, I have found it more convenient to use the counter space on the island directly behind the oven. For me it is simple to take a hot dish out of the oven, turn around without any extra steps, and put it on the ceramic tile countertop.

The cooktop needs counter space on each side, with 18 inches per side the bare minimum recommended by kitchen planners, but that is not enough. Thirty-six inches is preferable, at least on one side as that allows space for ingredients and utensils used in cooking — a plate or spoon holder to hold spoons and tongs, a place to put a hot pot after it is removed from the burner, and even a space for a cookbook standing in a plastic holder.

Adding salt and pepper or a dash of chili powder to the cooking is easy when spices are stored in a cabinet or drawer near the cooktop. Oils and condiments used most often in cooking are more convenient stored in the cooking center.

Storage space for pots, pans. and other cooking utensils should be in or adjacent to the cooking area. Since many of these can be rather weighty, roll-out shelves in base cabinets around the cooking area are a good storage space. An attractive rack above the cooktop is an ideal way to display your favorite pots and pans and is also a handy storage space. Famous chefs do it that way, why shouldn't you? Keep in mind, however, overhead racks are dust catchers. Also, it means that you have to keep your pots and pans sparkling clean.

If your cooktop is located in an island or peninsula and the other side is used for eating, the beginning or back of the eating area should be at least 12 inches, preferably more, from the back or side edge of the cooktop. This is to prevent the diners from being splattered by cooking and from inhaling cooking fumes.

Ranges or cooktops should not be placed under a window because of drafts and possible blowing curtains. The cooktop should also not be placed close to a doorway where there is traffic. Some like a cooktop against a wall, others prefer it in an island or peninsula where they do not have a closed in feeling.

Wall ovens can look attractive when placed at an angle across the corner of the kitchen, but this arrangement takes up valuable space particularly in a small kitchen.

THE CLEANUP AREA

The third major area in a kitchen is the cleanup center, which is the most often used part of the kitchen. Not only is it used for cleanup after meals but also for food preparation. Fruits and vegetables should be washed before cutting and dicing, and hands are constantly being washed or rinsed after each stage of food preparation. If I am preparing a dessert or anything else sweet, I cannot work with sticky fingers, so I am constantly washing my hands. The sink is most important to me as is a nearby towel rack.

The dishwasher should be installed next to the sink in the cleanup area, and if a trash compactor is used it should be on the other side of the sink, if space permits. If you are right-handed the dishwasher should be to the left of the sink, and if you are left-handed it should be to the right. There should be at least 40 inches in front of the closed dishwasher so that when it is open it will not impede the flow of traffic. If you load the dishwasher from the front allow an extra foot of space for traffic flow.

The configuration of the sinks is an individual preference. Whether a double sink, a larger single sink, or a sink with an attached drainboard is best left up to each cook and his or her style of food preparation and cleanup.

If you have a double or triple sink arrangement the placement of the disposal must be considered. Into which sink will you scrape the vegetable and fruit cuttings and which sink will you use to rinse your dishes? Although it was recommended to me that I place the disposal in the small vegetable sink, I chose to put in the big 10-inch deep sink, because that is where I scrape, rinse, and soak my dishes.

Another fairly new innovation is the instant hot water attachment, which is a spigot that when turned on provides 190 degree F. hot water instantly. The water is heated by a separate unit installed underneath the sink. This hot water spigot is wonderful for rinsing and heating serving plates, providing hot water for cooking, and for instant hot beverage preparation. I have also found that the heater under the sink makes this cabinet a warm place to raise bread dough.

Everyday glasses, dishes, and serving utensils should be stored near the cleanup area. It is ideal if this storage area is also in close proximity to the dining area. In that way dishes can be removed from the dishwasher, placed into storage, and within a short distance be used to set the dining table. We built a cabinet with two-sided sliding glass doors on top of the peninsula dividing the kitchen and breakfast area for this purpose. The clean dishes are placed into the cabinet on one side and later removed from the other to set the table.

Seldom-used dinnerware can be stored further away from the cleanup area. In our kitchen we built a floor to ceiling cabinet located beside the door to the dining room for our "good" china.

A cleanup area needs soap powders, dishwashing liquid, soaps, sponges, and other cleanup equipment and these should be stored either under the sink or in a nearby cabinet. Most cooks store cleaning equipment and a garbage pail under the sink. Many cabinets have a pull-out garbage pail or facility to hold garbage bags attached to the door of the cabinet under the sink.

Another feature recently added to under-the-sink cabinets is a narrow pull-out slanted compartment or tray just below the sink to hold sponges and other small cleaning equipment. I have this and have never used it, because I do not think a sponge or cloth dries well in a closed space cabinet. I have found a small compartmentalized plastic tray which holds a bottle of dishwashing liquid, a bottle of liquid hand soap, and a sponge. Since I clean up after each food preparation, I keep this tray beside the sink and always have the basic cleanup tools handy.

There are no rules as to where a sink should be placed other than its relationship to the other kitchen activity centers. It is not always necessary to place the sink under the window. That rule probably goes back to the time before electricity and dishwashers. People doing dishes wanted the natural light and also wanted something pleasant to look at when doing this mundane chore. It is still a desirable location, although not essential. Sinks can be placed in islands, peninsulas, or beneath cabinets.

Some kitchen designers recommend that corner sinks not be used in small kitchens because of loss of counter space. I had a corner sink in the apartment we rented and from experience I do not believe that placing it along a straight wall would have made that much difference in space. Besides, the corner placement of the sink in that situation added a certain charm to an otherwise mundane kitchen.

THE COLD STORAGE AREA

The refrigerator/freezer used to be the key component in the preparation area. Although still considered important in the basic kitchen work triangle, the refrigerator area is now considered a separate entity.

Some experts believe that it is ideal to have the refrigerator and pantry in close proximity to each

Baking center is lower than normal counter height for ease of rolling dough. Polo style laminated cabinets by Kraft Maid. Photo courtesy of Kraft Maid.

Baking center designed by Whirlpool and Better Homes and Gardens. There is sufficient room to roll out pie crusts and knead dough. The baking center is close to the ovens, microwave oven, and refrigerator. Appliances by Whirlpool. Photo courtesy of Whirlpool.

other with counter space in between. In that way the groceries that are unloaded on the counter can be quickly stored in their proper place. It is also convenient to have this center near the door through which the groceries are brought into the kitchen.

I planned my dream kitchen so that I could use the center island for unloading the grocery bags. The refrigerator is at one end of the island and the pantry at the other. With this large counter space in between I can quickly unpack all of the grocery bags, separate the refrigerator items from the pantry items, and put them away.

Although most kitchen planning books recommend 18 inches of counter space on the opening side of the refrigerator, I have found that is not enough to unload four large bags of groceries. Thirty inches is more practical, and then that area can also be used for food preparation.

THE BAKING AREA

The size and amount of counter space in the kitchen will determine whether you can have a separate baking area or use the food preparation area for baking.

Ideally the counter space you use as your baking center should be lower than the rest of the counters. It makes rolling dough so much easier and not as hard on your back. I decided not to have a separate baking center and use one long side of the island near the ovens for baking. The area is close to the pantry and baking utensils are stored underneath the counter.

If you have a definite baking center in your kitchen, you might want to build a marble slab for rolling out pastry dough into the countertop. Baking supplies, such as canisters of flour and sugar, extracts, baking powder, and molasses should be stored near the baking center. Your mix-master should be stored in this area, either on the counter, on a pull-out shelf, or on a shelf which pulls out and raises to counter height. With the latter you do not have to move the appliance to use it. Spatulas, rol-

ling pin, and other small baking equipment should also be stored in either drawers or cabinets in the baking area.

A vertically divided cupboard nearby is convenient for storing baking and cookie sheets. Any extra space in the cabinet can be used for tray storage. Other cake and bread pans should also be stored nearby. In organizing your baking pan storage try to nest as many of these as possible to save storage space. If you do a lot of baking you will find that various sizes of springform pans, tart pans, and pie pans nest well.

The baking center, particularly if it has a marble slab, is also an ideal place to make and roll pasta dough. If you have a bread machine, it too can be used in the baking center. However, the bread machine, which is self-contained, is an appliance that can be used anywhere in the kitchen.

THE HOSPITALITY AREA

If you have a large family or if you entertain frequently, a bar and drink preparation area, located in an out-of-the-way part of the kitchen, can alleviate traffic problems in the kitchen. In that way, the drink maker of the family is not using the main sink while you are trying to drain the pasta.

The bar and drink preparation area should include a small bar sink and at least a 30-inch counter space. Under-counter cabinets should provide storage for liquor and mixers. Keep in mind that if you decide to install a small refrigerator and a separate ice maker under the counter, in addition to the bar sink, you will need about 6 feet of counter and cabinet space.

In the cabinet above the sink and counter you will want storage for glasses, coasters, small snack trays, and condiments that do not require refrigeration.

The small bar sink does not have to be relegated just to drink preparation. The area makes a handy additional work surface and cleanup area for a second cook. If you are a flower arranger you can also use the small sink for this activity and store vases, candles, and other equipment underneath the counter, space permitting.

PLANNING AREA

Another activity area you might want to include in your kitchen is a planning area, which should be located in the quietest part of your dream kitchen where you can plan your meals, answer the phone, and even do some of the house bookkeeping.

The main component of the planning center is a desk with a file drawer and a shelf or two for cookbooks. The desk can be a knee-hole type with one or two banks of drawers, it can be a part of the kitchen counter with a high stool, or it can be a dropleaf shelf against a kitchen wall. When planning menus at your desk you will want a recipe index either in a file box, in a notebook, or on a computer. The planning center can be conveniently located at the end of a section of work cabinets or in a secluded alcove.

If the desk in your planning center is the knee-hole type it should have a drawer for office supplies and a file drawer that will conveniently hold folders with recipe clippings. The shallow top drawer of the desk can be divided with wooden slats to hold 3 × 5-inch recipe cards; this is handier than numerous recipe boxes.

The planning desk in the kitchen can also serve as a communication center. A telephone, placed either on top of the desk or on the wall near it, is convenient for outgoing and incoming calls without taking you away from the kitchen. If the telephone is installed on the wall it should be at a comfortable height to be used when sitting or standing. A message board for the family could be placed near the telephone. You might also want an intercom to keep track of family members throughout the house. This can be installed in the same area either on the desk or on the wall near it.

If you do extensive correspondence or other writing you might want a typewriter or computer on the desk. However, if the desk is near the cooking or cleanup area, it is not advisable to put a computer on it since heat, moisture, and smoke can damage it. I recently purchased a small portable laptop computer which is wonderful for recording recipes and cooking notations without leaving the kitchen.

Desks are usually 20 inches in depth, but if you want to keep in line with your base cabinets make the desk 24 inches deep which makes a more spacious desk top. The ideal height of a desk top is 30 inches. I recently saw a 36-inch high desk with a marble top and a stool. When not used for planning, the desk surface doubled as a part of the baking center.

The preferable desk length is 48 inches so that you can spread out several cookbooks on top of it while doing meal planning. However, if space is tight you can make the desk shorter by eliminating the side drawers and having only a single flat drawer underneath the desk top.

Regardless of what type of space you have for a planning center in your kitchen you should have at least a shelf or two for your favorite cookbooks. There is nothing like being in the middle of a recipe you thought was familiar to you, finding that you cannot remember all of its ingredients, and then having to go to another room to search for a cookbook. Although we know our everyday recipes by heart, it is a good idea to have the backup handy.

4
Kitchen Plans

Although the work triangle has been modified by usage over the years, its basic components still remain the most efficient kitchen design. The work triangle is still used for the most popular kitchen layouts, which are the one-wall, the galley, the U-shaped, the L-shaped, and the island designs.

The shape of the room also influences the kitchen arrangement. A long narrow room lends itself to a galley kitchen, a rectangular room to an L-shaped kitchen, and a square room to a U-shaped kitchen.

In all of these kitchen layouts, traffic flow is a major consideration. The most desirable kitchen is one that allows the rest of the members of the household to flow in and out of the kitchen without interfering with the cook. Granted, family members may want to get a cold drink from the refrigerator or use the microwave oven to prepare a snack, but the kitchen should be designed to minimize interference from these activities with those of the family cook.

Most kitchen plans avoid having the main flow of traffic going through the work triangle. In large kitchens a center island helps to prevent such traffic.

THE ONE-WALL KITCHEN

The single wall kitchen lines up all of the appliances and work centers on one wall. Many times this kitchen arrangement is part of another room, such as a living area, and it is also often used in small apartments or vacation homes.

The one-wall kitchen is considered to be the least efficient as far as the work triangle is concerned, because it requires extra steps between the two furthest points of the triangle. However, it has been found that it is the most efficient use of space in a small kitchen. Also, the straight lines created by such an arrangement can visually enlarge the room.

The one-wall kitchen is most efficient when the sink is located between the refrigerator and the range. If possible there should be at least 3 feet of counter space between the sink and the appliances on either side of it. A roll-around cart with a butcher block, tiled, or laminated top can be helpful as an additional work area.

Traffic flow is not a problem in this kitchen since most of the traffic is in the living area behind the cook.

THE GALLEY KITCHEN

The galley or corridor kitchen is usually the smallest of all kitchen designs. It is compact and would remind you of its namesake — the galley of a ship. Just because this kitchen is small does not mean that it is not functional or is incomplete. However, if you desire this type of kitchen you must make every inch of space count.

In planning a galley kitchen try to place the cooktop, sink, and dishwasher on the longest wall, with the refrigerator and food storage cabinets almost directly opposite. This eliminates excess steps and makes the kitchen function more efficiently. However, some kitchen designers prefer the refrigerator and sink on one wall and the range

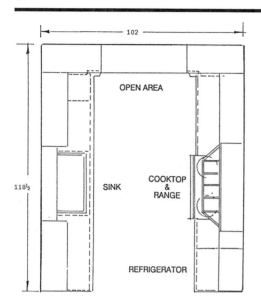

The galley kitchen. Plan courtesy of Wood-Mode.

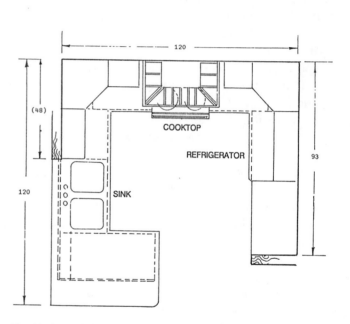

The U-shaped kitchen. Plan courtesy of Wood-Mode.

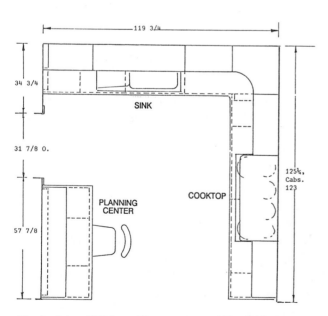

The L-shaped kitchen. Plan courtesy of Wood-Mode.

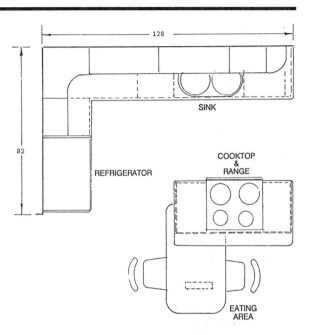

A compact kitchen with an island that houses a drop-in range. An eating area is attached to the island. Plan courtesy of Wood-Mode.

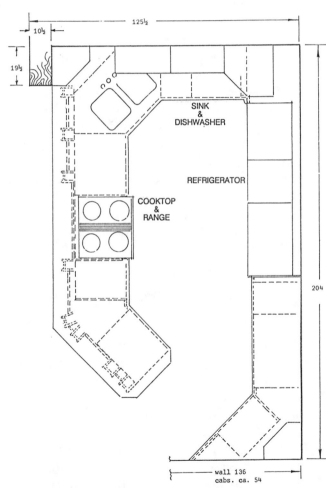

A long peninsula is connected to a permanent wall. The sink is installed catty-corner, and the cooktop is located in the peninsula. Plan courtesy of Wood-Mode.

or cooktop and ovens on the other wall. Regardless of which arrangement you prefer, the aisle between the two rows of counters should be no less than 4 feet and no more than 6 feet. There should also be 3 feet of counter space between the two major components of the triangle located on the same wall.

It is almost impossible to keep traffic from coming through this type of kitchen, since it is a galley. If the kitchen is a main thoroughfare through the house you should have a 6 foot maximum between counters. This will allow for the refrigerator door to be open while someone is passing through.

Since the galley kitchen is a very basic cooking environment, it should be decorated simply so that it will not have a cluttered look. White, pastel, or light wood such as pickled oak gives a fresh and airy feeling to cabinets. Countertops as well as the back splash should also be in a light tone. The floor can either blend or contrast with the countertops or cabinets, but in any event should have easy upkeep since there is considerable traffic in this type of kitchen.

An interesting effect can be created in a galley kitchen when the kitchen is combined with an adjoining family room if one upper wall of the kitchen is left open. Thus the base cabinets of the open wall become a peninsula divider for the family room. A dropped part of the peninsula on the family room side can serve as the eating area, and either the cooktop or sink can be installed in the raised part of the peninsula.

THE L-SHAPED KITCHEN

In the L-shaped kitchen, the major work areas which form a triangle are along two walls of the kitchen. Although this plan permits flexibility in the arrangement of the work areas, it is most efficient if the work flows from refrigerator to sink, to cooking and serving areas. If it is not in that order, you will probably be taking extra steps.

The L-shaped kitchen takes less space than the U-shaped one and can be almost as efficient.

THE U-SHAPED KITCHEN

Many kitchen designers agree that the U-shaped kitchen is the most efficient, since it has three walls for storage and work space which are out of the normal flow of household traffic. Traffic passing through the kitchen flows along the open part of the U and does not interfere with the work triangle. To provide work-counter space and a minimum of 4 feet between work centers, you will need at least 8 feet on the base of the U.

The U-shaped kitchen usually has one of the major work areas on each wall and the combined sides of the work triangle should total between 12 and 22 feet. If smaller, your kitchen is probably cramped and if larger, you are taking unnecessary steps in your daily kitchen duties.

A C-shaped kitchen with cabinets and appliances on three walls is another version of the U-shaped kitchen with smaller side walls. For more efficiency, either the sink or a free-standing range could be placed in the corner at an angle, however, this gives a smaller appearance to the kitchen. If space permits, an island can be placed at the open part of the C to give more work space and create a more efficient work triangle. As an alternative, a moveable island can be placed along the fourth wall.

THE BROKEN L- OR U-SHAPED KITCHEN

While not the most desirable configuration, the broken L- or U-shaped kitchen is frequently necessary to provide access to adjoining rooms. This configuration is a common necessity when expanding a kitchen in an older home.

The broken L- or U-shaped kitchen can present traffic problems, particularly if the U is broken by a doorway. A broken U-shaped kitchen interrupts the continuous flow of countertops and cabinets, making the kitchen less efficient.

However, this type of kitchen can work to advantage by providing individual work space for a two cook family.

PENINSULAS AND ISLANDS

The peninsula attaches at a right angle to a wall or a bank of cabinets. It is as versatile and as practical as an island but does not require as much total floor space, since an aisle is eliminated on one short side. The peninsula is usually designed to act as a divider between the kitchen and breakfast area or family room. If a cooktop or sink is placed in the peninsula, it enables the cook to socialize while she is cooking.

If the peninsula incorporates a sink or cooktop, it should be at least 6½ feet from the wall (i.e., 2 feet of wall counter and 4½ feet of peninsula) and 3 feet wide. This suggested length is shorter than the space required for an island with either a sink or cooktop since the adjacent wall counter can also be used. When using the back side of the peninsula as an eating area another 1½ feet should be added to the width.

An island in a kitchen can be one of the most used and attractive areas of the kitchen. It can shorten the distance between work areas and can act as a buffer to traffic passing through the kitchen. An island can add counter and storage space and often serves as the home for a sink and dishwasher, or cooktop and modular grill. It is also a center for family and friends to chat with the cook and participate in food preparations.

The island can be as short as 4 feet and still contain drawers and cabinets of various dimension. However, it should be at least 6 feet long in order to accommodate either a cooktop or sink and have sufficient counter space to surround either one. It should be at least 3 feet wide. An island can act as a divider in a large kitchen and give the cook different areas for various cooking tasks. I use different sides of my island for various work areas — cooking at the cooktop, as a bake center, and for food preparation.

Islands can house either the main sink or a smaller one. If the main sink is placed in the island the dishwasher should be next to it. Many people like the main sink in the island because it lets the cook work and talk with those around her at the same time. Allow at least 18 inches of counter space on one side of the sink and 24 inches on the other.

However, before placing the main sink in the island, consider the fact that the island is the focal point of the room. You may not want to highlight your dream kitchen with a sink full of dirty dishes. Since my island is a gathering point for guests I opted to have the cooktop in the island.

Cooktops with downdraft venting systems made islands popular. However, cooktops can be installed in an island with an overhead ventilation system hidden in an overhead hood, which can be a decorative enhancement to a large kitchen. In a small kitchen such a hood can be overpowering, however.

If you are using a downdraft system with your cooktop and want a decorative accent over the island, you can use still use a hood or an attractive pot rack, either in a modern or traditional decor. Chantal, the cookware manufacturer, has recently introduced a hanging grid design pot rack with a unique light track bar to spotlight the work area on the island. It is constructed of heavy gauge steel with either a white or chrome rim.

If the cooktop is placed in the island there should be a minimum of 12 inches of counter space on one side and 18 inches on the other. I prefer 24 inches on one side and 36 inches on the other. A central island can also house a drop-in range. If you use additional small electrical cooking appliances on the island, you should provide electrical outlets for their use. Determine on which area of the island you will use them and place the outlets accordingly. I found it best to have the electrical outlets on the solid ends of the island.

An island can be designed with seating space for breakfast, lunch, and even informal entertaining. An overhanging counter from an island makes a good informal eating area. If the eating area shares the island with the main sink or cooktop, consider lowering the counter to create a second level at the same 30 inch height as a dining table or lowering the cooktop in the island. Using one part

The center island is large enough for the cooktop and various food preparation activities. Appliances by KitchenAid. Photo courtesy of KitchenAid.

of the island as a dining area in a small kitchen can provide dining space which otherwise might not be available.

The free-standing island does not necessarily have to conform to the rest of the kitchen. However, if it does conform, multiple units of stock cabinets of varying widths can be used to form an island. A butcher block cart or even a large antique table can be used as an island. The latter must be set on a 6-inch base so as to bring it up to counter height.

The shape of the island, however, does not have to be limited to squares or rectangles. The ends might be rounded to handle traffic flow more efficiently. Islands can also be round or octagonal and do not have to be perpendicular to cabinets.

The countertop material of a kitchen island does not have to match the rest of the countertops in the kitchen. The choice of materials for the top of the island is wide. Laminates are easy to clean; tile which has grout lines is basically heat resistant; granite is durable, heat resistant, and has few seam lines. A butcher block is not recommended around a sink because it will stain. You might choose to use a variety of materials for different parts of the island such as marble for the baking area, butcher block for chopping in the preparation area, and tile or granite around the sink or cooktop. Granite can also be used in the baking area.

Lighting for an island can be hanging lights for a soft effect or ceiling spots to illuminate individual work areas or both. I find the spotlights (or bullets) good for task lighting on my island and enjoy two hanging Tiffany lamps at the ends for softer light.

In planning an island for your kitchen be sure to leave enough space around it for traffic flow and to allow cabinet, dishwasher, and refrigerator doors to be opened. Four-foot wide aisles are recommended, but may be cut to 36 or 42 inches in an unusual situation. We have a variety of clearance around our island — 4½ feet in the main traffic area, 4 feet between the refrigerator and the island, and 4 feet on the two long work sides.

THE UNUSUAL SHAPED KITCHEN

As you look around you will find many varia-tions of the basic kitchen designs. Most of them do conform to the ideas of the basic work triangle.

For example, a friend combined a peninsula with an island to create a most efficient kitchen. One short wall of her kitchen houses the refrigerator and a built-in oven. A drop-in downdraft range is centered in the peninsula. The L-shaped island opposite the peninsula houses a full-size sink used for food preparation. On the aisle side of the island there is a rounded overhanging lip used for informal dining. The other short wall of the kitchen contains a planning center, another full size sink, and a dishwasher. Since this area is adjacent to the dining room it is ideal for cleanup. Behind the long side of the island below a bank of windows there are shelves for cookbooks.

There is no reason you cannot design your kitchen the way you want it. The plan does not have to conform to the work triangle which was conceived forty years ago, when there were no cooktops, no wall ovens, few dishwashers, no trash compactors, and few refrigerator/freezer combinations. The kitchen is your domain — design it, work in it, and live in it according to the style that is most efficient and pleasurable to you. I enjoy cooking, find it relaxing, and have designed my kitchen to please me.

5
Cooking Appliances

INTRODUCTION TO MAJOR APPLIANCES

The Computer Age of the 1980s has made our major appliances more user-friendly with touch control panels, more energy efficient, and more diversified in energy options. Appliances are now offered with a gas and electric cooktop combination, or a microwave and convection oven combination. Today's appliances are designed to coordinate and integrate with modern kitchens, regardless of whether they are traditional, contemporary, or modern in decor.

European appliances have had a strong influence on American designs. The European sleek, built-in look has been copied by many American manufacturers. European appliance manufacturers were the innovators of cast iron solid element disks on cooktops and the dotted surfaces on the smooth ceramic glass cooktops — both revolutionary in the use of cooking energy and the appearance of the cooktop.

Products from the major appliance manufacturers fall into three price groupings. The first grouping is that of the affordable models for the mass market, the second is the more expensive models with more convenience features, and the third grouping, which has appeared most recently, includes appliances with yet more convenience features and the most up-to-date styling. The latter is aimed at the top 10 to 20% of the market.

Several of the major U.S. appliance manufacturers produce products in all three categories. For example, General Electric's Hotpoint line is aimed

toward the mass market, its General Electric line is the higher end, and the Monogram series is targeted to the customers who want and can afford a custom-kitchen look. KitchenAid is the custom line of the Whirlpool Corporation, and the Elite line serves the same purpose for Frigidaire, a division of White Consolidated Industries.

The Raytheon Company, which originated microwave ovens, has created a three-in-one Cook-'N-Clean Center through its Modern Maid appliance division. The 30-inch built-in kitchen appliance combines cooking and cleaning and is ideal for a small kitchen. The compact unit has an eye level gas or electric 21-inch continuous cleaning oven, a gas or electric cooktop, and a 12-place setting capacity dishwasher in the base.

Electronic circuitry in today's major kitchen appliances has made them easier to operate by touch control and provided a number of pre-programmed settings. The electronics also provide built-in safeguards to prevent users from putting together incompatible functioning cycles. In addition, electronics provide continuous information to let the user know whether the appliance is functioning correctly or whether there is a problem. As with any electronic device, it takes a while to learn to understand and use the controls.

According to Whirlpool engineers, electronic components in appliances are just beginning. In the home of the future, appliances will be voice-activated and they will be able to speak with synthetic speech. Appliances will be able to be operated by a home computer and even remotely

MA-1 Modern Maid's Cook'-B-Clean Center with oven, cooktop, and dishwasher in a 30-inch unit. Photo courtesy of Modern Maid.

through the use of the telephone. That is all well and good, but I do not think I am ready for an oven or a refrigerator that talks back to me!

CHOOSING COOKING APPLIANCES

Regardless of whether you spend a great deal of time in the kitchen cooking or are there just long enough to heat something in the microwave, there is a cooking appliance for you. In the past two decades new cooking methods have become popular, such as magnetic-induction, microwave, halogen, and convection cooking. Many of these methods provide high heat speedily and are also capable of cooking at a very low temperature. With some cooktop units it is possible to mix energy options and cooking components to fit your needs.

Although when purchasing a new cooking appliance the cooking features are of prime concern, it is also important to consider the style and color of the appliance. Today it is possible to find styles and colors to match any decor and size of your kitchen.

Cooking units are available either built-in or free-standing. Built-in appliances usually create a sleeker, more sophisticated design, although many free-standing units can be "dropped" into place and made to look like built-ins. The built-ins are more expensive and installation labor adds to their cost.

Before choosing a range, cooktop, or ovens, however, you have to decide which type of cooking you prefer — gas, electricity, or a combination of the two. For instance, if you choose to have built-ins, you could have gas for the cooktop and electricity for the ovens. Some cooktops even have a combination of the two. Most of the special features are available for either energy option.

RANGES

A free-standing range rests on the floor and contains a cooktop, usually with four burners, two 6-inch and two 8-inch, and an oven below. Some units include an upper oven at eye level which is often a microwave, as well as a built-in ventilation system. The slide-in range is also free-standing and fully insulated, but does not have side panels and thus has to fit snugly between cabinets. A drop-in range, on the other hand, does not reach the floor and is a built-in that is installed in the cabinets on a specially constructed base cabinet which has a kickplate and may have a drawer. All of these ranges include a cooktop and an oven underneath. Most of these units are 30 inches wide and fit into the standard 36-inch high countertop.

However, there are smaller and larger models such as the 20-inch electric or gas range by Whirlpool with one 8-inch and three 6-inch burners. The company also makes two 40-inch models, each

Jenn-Air drop-in 30-inch Grill-Range with downdraft ventilation has four types of plug-in cooktop cartridges, a conventional oven which can be switched to convection, and electronic controls. Photo courtesy of Jenn-Air.

Whirlpool's all white 30-inch set-in range with solid element cooktop. Photo courtesy of Whirlpool.

with a large and a small oven, plus two 6-inch burners and two 8-inch burners.

The term eye-level or bi-level ranges refers to ranges that have four burners and an upper and lower oven. In the gas units the upper ovens use gas energy and in the electric models the upper ovens are microwaves. Many of these ranges also have an updraft ventilation system and some have a storage drawer underneath the bottom oven. The bi-level ranges are excellent space savers. If you use tall stock pots for cooking make sure there is enough room between the cooktop and upper oven for these pots.

There are also free-standing and slide-in ranges with downdraft ventilation systems, and modular cooking units, such as grills, griddles, and rotisseries. These units also give you a choice of burners ranging from radiant, high speed coil, or solid elements (for definition, see Electric Cook-tops, this chapter).

Many ranges have electronic programming and precise temperature controls. Oven functions, such as delayed start and self-cleaning, are con-trolled by touching the electronic control panel.

Other features of today's ranges include self-cleaning or continuous clean ovens, electronic clock/timer controls for the ovens, and illuminated see-through oven doors. White or black tempered glass oven doors are matched with white, black, almond, or stainless steel exteriors on these ranges.

Examples of some of the latest features in ranges are as follows:

- Whirlpool's new all white drop-in 30-inch range has a white glass solid-element cooktop with cooking controls on the right side. The oven con-trols on the front of the range include an elec-tronic MEALTIMER™ clock.

- Magic Chef makes a combination built-in gas cooktop with an electric oven underneath.

- Amana's new free standing range has 6-inch and 8-inch quartz halogen (for definition, see Electric Cooktops, this chapter) elements, two electric resistance elements, and a self-cleaning oven.

- General Electric's White-on-White line features a 30-inch free-standing gas range with spill-proof burners and a self-cleaning oven. Some models have an automatic pilotless ignition, white porcelain enamel cooktop, square burner grates, a white glass oven door with a window, digital clock, automatic oven timer, and a large storage drawer.

- Modern Maid has introduced its first electric downdraft ranges. They are free-standing with full width ovens, and come with five interchangeable cooktop cartridges for grill, griddle, and cooking elements in either solid disk or black ceramic glass.

- Frigidaire makes cleanup of their cooktops easy since the entire cooktop lifts up and out of the way for easy cleaning. The backdrop of the cooktop is seamless and thus does not trap dirt or grease.

- Jenn-Air makes both downdraft and updraft free-standing or built-in ranges. Most of the units have interchangeable modules, such as a grill, griddle, wok, and steamer as well as a choice of conventional, glass-ceramic, solid element, or induction burners.

- Jenn-Air's new Dual-Fuel™ grill range has a gas cooktop, an electric oven, and a downdraft ventilation system. The 30-inch wide appliance combines indoor grilling with gas cooking. The grill module can be replaced with additional burners, a griddle, or a wok. The oven can be switched from conventional baking to convection with the turn of a dial. The unit can be installed as a built-in, or with side panels and backsplash as a free-standing unit.

Commercial-Type Cookstoves for Home Use

Many cooking aficionados prefer a commercial gas range, or the next best thing to it — a commercial gas range manufactured for home use. These cooks claim that this type of range produces more even heat. However, a true commercial range must be kept at a constant temperature all day to produce optimum results. The genuine commercial ranges are bigger, heavier, and produce a great deal more heat than either gas or electric home ranges. They require special installation, should be free-standing to allow for heat circulation, and must be placed on a reinforced, heat-resistant floor. Commercial restaurant-type ranges tend to make the kitchen hot in summer.

Several manufacturers such as Viking, Thermador, Wolf, Garland, and AGA produce commercial-type ranges that have been adapted to residential use. Depending on the model, these ranges have six or eight burners; one, two, or three ovens; a broiler; and a built-in grill.

For example, Garland makes a 60-inch commercial-type gas range for the home, which features six burners with electronic ignition, two super-size ovens, and a 24-inch built-in heavy-duty griddle. The burners are a starburst design for even heat-distribution under both large and small cooking utensils. The griddle has a broiler rack underneath it. The 36-inch gas range also has six burners, but only one oven and no griddle. However, a griddle is optional for the cooktop, replacing two of the burners.

AGA, an acronym for Amalgamated Gas Accumulator, is a British manufacturer of a unique commercial-type range designed for home use. Invented in 1922 by Swedish Nobel Prize winning physicist Gustaf Dalen, the AGA range operates on the principle of stored heat — consequently it is left on all the time. A single central gas-fired burner, similar to a pilot light, distributes heat to seven separate cooking areas. Each of the cooking areas has a specific function and emits constant heat.

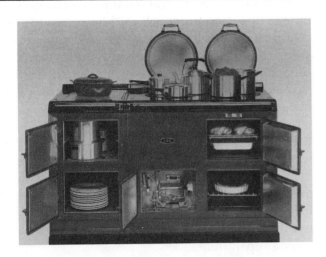

AGA cookstove with four burners, a boiling plate, a simmering plate, and a warming plate. Photo courtesy of AGA.

There are no knobs to turn, no dials to set, and no ovens or burners to preheat.

The AGA cook stove has four ovens and three surface cooking areas, each of which operates at a preset temperature. One surface area is set for boiling, another for simmering, and the third for warming. They are covered with insulating lids when not in use. The ovens are set to either bake, roast, simmer, or warm. Since this method of cooking involves the use of pre-set temperatures, cooking utensils must be moved, therefore, from one area or oven to another during various stages of cooking. The AGA cookstoves are available in four and in two-oven models as well as in seven color combinations. The AGA cookstove must be installed by a trained AGA craftsman and requires external venting.

Old-Fashioned Cookstoves

Some homeowners are once again using the old-fashioned cookstoves that were popular in the late 1800s and early 1900s. These cookstoves are available as either restored originals or as antique reproductions. The vintage wood- and coal-burning stoves add warmth to the kitchen during the cold winter months and therefore are popular in the northern states. Many of these old coal- and wood-burning stoves are very ornate and add charm to a country kitchen.

Although not as ornate, the gas cookstoves of the 1920s and '30s are also popular. They are roomy and provide many features. They have anywhere from four to six burners and from two to four ovens plus a warming drawer. Maybe not as efficient as our modern gas cooktops, they are highly sought after by cooks who want an old-fashioned kitchen.

There is an enormous variety of old-fashioned cookstoves — both antique and reproductions. The antique stoves come in wood-, coal-, and gas-burning models, with some units even using a combination of fuels. Reproduction models are also available using a combination of fuels. Electric models of reproductions of old stoves are also being made. The Elmira Stove Works of Ontario, Canada makes one of the widest selections of reproduction stoves. The Bryant Stove Works in Thorndike, Maine offers a catalog of stoves, and The Antique Stove Association offers a list of nationwide antique cookstove dealers and restorers. The Cumberland General Store in Tennessee sells six antique stove reproductions from various manufacturers.

The most well-known of the above resources is the Elmira Stove Works of Ontario, Canada which makes four types of reproduction free-standing cookstoves — gas, electric, wood-burning, and a combination wood and electric stove. Both gas and electric models have a built-in exhaust fan. The gas model has six burners and the electric has four with one being a 10-inch element suited for large pots and pans. On the electric cooktop there is also a large rectangular cooking element, which is ideal for a large roaster or a griddle pan. Both models have large ovens and storage space for pots and pans.

The Elmira Stove Works also has two models which burn either coal or wood. These have six

The Elmira Stove Works reproduction gas stove features six burners, a large oven, and storage drawers. Photo courtesy of The Elmira Stove Works.

them. Many cooktops come with various convertible cartridges such as a grill, griddle, wok, and even a deep soup kettle or steamer. These cooking accessories are very easy to install and give a versatility to cooking. With these convertible cartridges you can easily turn out a large batch of pancakes or grill four to six steaks.

Today's cooktops are very versatile in the type of energy source. Gas and electric modules can even be installed side by side in the same unit, provided the proper piping and wiring are available. The combination of gas and electric burners lets the cook use the former for sautéing and frying, and the latter for simmering, stewing, and delicate sauce preparations.

There is a large variety of cooktops available — from two to six burners. There is even a one burner electric induction cooktop from General Electric, which can easily be stored when not in use. General Electric and Dacor make an electric cooktop with the fifth burner designed especially for low heat cooking.

square feet of cooking surface, a large oven, and a warming cabinet. The combination wood-burning and electric range has a cast iron cooking surface in addition to solid element electric burners. The oven is electric. The wood-burning firebox not only provides energy for the cast iron cooking surface but also for home heating.

COOKTOPS

In recent years there have been more technological advances in cooktops than in any other kitchen appliance. There is not only a choice between gas and electric, but within the electric option, there is a choice of the type of burners or disks (they are called hobs in Europe).

With today's modular cooktops you can change your type of cooking according to your needs. The cooking surface can be customized with burner modules or accessories to replace

General Electric's five burner cooktop shown with grill module. The fifth burner in the center has the Sensi Temp II™ sensor, which monitors the temperature and electronically maintains the selected level of heat. Photo courtesy of General Electric.

General Electric's cooktop with the fifth burner includes a precision Sensi-Temp II™ sensor which monitors the temperature of the utensil and electronically maintains the selected heat level. The heat sensing device also has an audible boil detector which lets you know when the contents of the utensil have reached the boiling point.

High-powered burners, which heat quickly and will cook large amounts of food, are now included in many electric and gas cooktops. New non-stick material on the burners and cooktop make cleaning easy.

Although cooktops can be placed almost anywhere in the kitchen, it is important to check some of the features before installation. You should consider where the pot handles will be when the cooktop is in use. Pot handles should never jut into a traffic lane, extend across a burner, or obstruct the control knobs. Staggered cooking elements in a cooktop with controls in the front make reaching the two back burners easier than if they are one behind the other.

Also, when choosing a built-in cooktop, check to see where the controls are located. If they are along or toward the back, you may have to reach over a steaming pot to use them. Many cooktops have the controls located in the center toward the front, others have controls along one side, or in a front panel. My General Electric built-in cooktop has electronic controls on the front which eliminates touching the cooktop for any heat adjustments.

Some cooktops consist of only two-burner cartridges which allow for the placement of these two-burner cartridges almost anywhere in the kitchen. Space permitting you might even want four burners or two cartridges in a row along the front of the counter instead of a grid with two in front and two in the back. This is ideal for handicapped people confined to a wheelchair who have difficulty reaching the back burners. These burner cartridges can also be placed in different areas of the kitchen to accommodate two cooks in the family.

Many cooktops have a downdraft ventilation system. This self-venting cooktop eliminates the need for a separate ventilation system with a hood, which can be obtrusive when installed over an island in a small kitchen. They are not as efficient, however, when tall cooking utensils must be used.

ELECTRIC COOKTOPS

In the past two decades there has been a great revolution in electric cooktops. They are more streamlined, more appropriate for today's kitchen designs, and they offer the cook a choice of four cooking surfaces — conventional coil, solid element, glass-ceramic, and induction, or a combination of two.

Although some of the first electric ranges built in the United States had solid elements, the coil type elements were more popular since they heated and cooked faster. In Europe, solid elements became the norm and over the years were greatly improved with higher wattage and thermal protectors. As interest in European kitchen design spread to this country, modern solid element cooktops were introduced.

When the first electric ranges were introduced in the 1890s there was also considerable experimentation with induction cooking but it was not accepted. However, the solid state circuitry developed in the 1970s and the glass-ceramic materials developed by the aerospace industry made induction cooking practical for home use.

Conventional Coils

Still the most common type of electric cooktops uses the conventional coils, which use electrical resistance to create heat. This method of cooking consists of wire encased in a metallic tube filled with an insulation material. The tube is bent into the shape of a coil which is flattened on top to provide maximum contact with the cooking utensil. The heat travels from the coil to the cookware by both conduction (where there is direct contact between the element and the pot or pan) and radiation.

Solid Elements

The solid elements are made of cast iron disks which conduct heat to the cookware. The underside of these disks contains electric resistant wires embedded in ceramic insulation. The disks are sealed into a cooktop made of tempered glass or enamel on steel.

Although the solid elements take somewhat longer to heat or cool than conventional coil burners, they retain heat well and provide even heat across the cooking surface. The solid elements provide a steady heat even at very low temperatures. Since the solid elements do retain heat and continue to cook, the elements can be turned off 5 to 10 minutes before the food is ready. However, they must also be given time to warm up to cooking temperature.

There are three types of solid elements available. One is equipped with a thermal protector, or limiter, which reduces the wattage to the element to prevent overheating. The second is thermostatically controlled with a thermostat in the center of the element that senses the temperature of the bottom of the pan. This element can be set for a range of temperatures between 150 degrees F. and 520 degrees F. General Electric, Dacor, and Frigidaire have this element in some of their cooktops. Thermador features thermostat controls that have twelve different settings from 145 degrees F. to 520 degrees F. The third type of element is a low wattage solid element without a thermal protector or a thermostat control. There is a boiling alarm built into some of the solid elements that sounds when the contents of the pan reaches the boiling temperature. If you follow the warning, messy boil-overs can be prevented.

Caloric, a division of the Raytheon Company, has recently introduced plug-in disk elements for their cooktops. With these plug-in disks you can convert the cooking elements from conventional coil to solid element cooking and back again.

Solid elements make cleanup easier. The solid elements are fitted without a seam into a tempered glass cooktop surface so that there is no need for a drip pan. The solid-element cooktops can be wiped clean with a damp cloth and soapy scouring pads can be used for heavy cleanup. However, be sure to heat the elements after a wet cleaning in order to prevent rust and corrosion.

Even though most of the tempered glass cooktops used with solid element disks are black, the recent interest in white kitchen appliances has spawned white glass cooktops by such manufacturers as Whirlpool, KitchenAid, Amana, and General Electric. KitchenAid has a 36-inch solid element cooktop with power track lines printed on the surface that light up when an element is in use.

For best cooking performance with solid-element cooktops, it is also important that the proper cookware is used. Only flat, heavy-gauge, smooth-bottomed pans should be used for maximum efficiency. The pans should not extend beyond the heating element by more than 1 inch.

Glass-ceramic Elements

The glass-ceramic cooktop and the induction cooktop have a glass-ceramic surface in common, which is usually separated from the countertop by a metal frame. Many of these cooktops are manufactured by Schott and are known as "ceran glass-ceramic." They are black, translucent, easy to clean, and fit almost any decor.

In a glass-ceramic cooktop the heat is radiated to the cooktop by heating elements (electric coils) underneath. Heat travels from the glass surface to the cookware primarily through conduction. The areas to be heated are indicated on the glass-ceramic by either circles, sunbursts, or lines. These indicators change color when the area is heated. Although the first of these ceramic-glass cooktops were white, they were changed to black, but now fashion has dictated a return to white.

Since the glass-ceramic cooktop provides a

Caloric's exclusive plug-in solid disk elements are interchangeable with conventional coil elements for flexibility in cooking. Photo courtesy of Caloric.

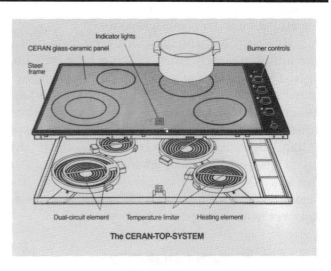

The ceran glass-ceramic cooktop system shows the cooking elements under the cooktop. Photo courtesy of Schott America.

continuous surface, wiping up spills from it is as easy as maintaining your countertops. The glass-ceramic finishes of these smooth-top elements are sturdy and scratch resistant. Some manufacturers say you can use a single edge razor blade to loosen cooked-on spills. When the burners are turned off, you have an extra work space.

For most efficient cooking, flat bottom pans are required for glass-ceramic cooktops.

Induction Heating

The induction cooktop is identical to the glass-ceramic cooktop in appearance but the cooking power and its function are entirely different. Induction coils, located underneath the glass-ceramic surface, generate heat in iron or steel (including enamel-coated steel) cooking containers by passing a magnetic field through them. This action agitates the molecules of the cooking utensil, which in turn produces heat. The heat is transferred to the food and cooks it in the same manner as do other conventional electric or gas cooktops. Since the cook-

ing utensil must have magnetic properties, a good test to see if you have the right pan is whether or not an ordinary household magnet will stick to it.

There are several other points to consider about induction cooktops. Like gas, these cooktops turn on and off instantly and can be set at very low heat for delicate cooking. Another advantage to induction cooking is that the glass-ceramic cooktop itself does not get hot. On the other hand, these cooktops are higher priced than the conventional ones. However, if you want one for special low heat cooking, consider the single induction unit by General Electric, mentioned above.

Halogen Heating

Halogen cooking is another new innovation. The burners are powered by two vacuum-sealed quartz-glass tubes filled with halogen gas. The gas quickly heats when electric current is passed through the tube. This heat is then transferred through the glass-ceramic cooktop and the energy instantly heats the cooking utensil. Halogen cooking has the quick response of induction heating and is more efficient to operate.

However, halogen cooktops are not inexpensive and that is why most cooktops have only one or two such elements with the rest being conventional electric heating. Gaggenau, the German appliance manufacturer, includes a halogen cooking zone on its glass-ceran cooktop which gives you instant high heat and can be lowered again with the same speed. Blanco has manufactured one of the first all halogen glass-ceramic cooktops. It is designed for short-period cooking and has a wide range of heat settings.

GAS COOKTOPS

Cooking with gas will probably remain a kitchen favorite forever. Gas is used by professional chefs, and most people say that once you've cooked with gas you will prefer it over electricity. Gas gives you instant heat and accurate temperature control (although electric elements can now be controlled to a wide range of temperatures).

Gas cooktops are available in multiple-burner units with many options. Most gas cooktops have either two, four, or six burners. High-powered gas cooktops are manufactured by Thermador and KitchenAid.

Many of the new gas cooking elements have energy-saving electronic ignitions rather than a pilot light. Thermador has an automatic re-ignition system called ThermaFlame™ which is designed to sense flame-outs and instantly re-lights the burners with an electric spark. Thermador gas cooktops are only three inches deep, which allows for more drawer space and cabinets underneath than is possible with many electric cooktops.

On many gas cooktops the jets are sealed into the surface, eliminating the need for drip pans. KitchenAid's 30- or 36-inch units have burners which are sealed in tempered glass and have pilotless electronic ignition.

Although decorative options are more limited with gas cooktops than with their electric counter-parts, there is still a great variety from which to choose. Gas cooktop surfaces are available in a number of attractive enamel colors, brushed chrome, and stainless steel. Some manufacturers, such as Dacor and General Electric, produce gas cooktops with glass-ceramic surfaces. General Electric's 5-burner gas Monogram cooktop also has a retractable downdraft venting hood that disappears when not in use.

Many of the electric and gas cooktops are available in a variety of colors. Dacor's six-burner gas model comes in a brilliant red, and General Electric's Monarch series comes in white. Many gas cooktops are also available in brushed chrome or black, the new fashion accent to the popular all-white kitchen.

MODULAR COOKTOPS

The development of the modular cooktop in both gas and electric energy brought a new dimension to cooking and to kitchen design. With multiple interchangeable modules, the modular cooktop can be a different appliance each time you use it. The modules are very easy to snap in and remove.

Not all manufacturers offer the same modules with their electric or gas cooktops. Some cooktops are standard with a two burners module and a grill. An additional two burners is considered an extra module. Many manufacturers of electric modular cooktops offer a variety of burners — conventional coil, solid element, glass-ceramic, or induction.

A modular cooktop, however, can also mean that only a part of the cooktop can be removed. For instance, Modern Maid's solid disk electric glass cooktop has a removable grill module that can be replaced with a griddle. The 42-inch unit also has two 6-inch and two 8-inch solid disk elements.

The standard modules offered by many cooktop manufacturers are a grill, rotisserie, and griddle. Other modules are a wok, a steamer, and a deep fat fryer. As previously mentioned, some cooktops have both electric and gas modules.

KitchenAid's tempered glass gas cooktop with sealed burners and pilotless electronic ignition for each burner. Photo courtesy of KitchenAid.

General Electric's Monogram five-burner gas cooktop with glass ceramic surface and retractable downdraft venting hood. Photo courtesy of General Electric.

The grill module allows you to grill indoors. This attachment requires a strong ventilation system and consequently many of the cooktops with this attachment have variable speed downdraft ventilation. The grill grates are often made with non-stick surfaces and there is also a drip pan underneath the grill. The rotisserie is attached to the grill module and includes skewers for kebabs.

The griddle has a large surface for preparing pancakes, or the like, for more than two people. It also has a removable grease drip pan and is usually made of a non-stick material for easy cleaning.

The deep fryer comes with a wire basket and is only available for electric cooktops. The cooker-steamer, which poaches, blanches, steams, and stews large quantities of foods, is also only available on electric models. The wok can be used only with conventional coil electric cooktops. Most of these accessory modules were pioneered by Jenn-Air.

There is great versatility in today's cooktops. Even Jenn-Air's basic 30-inch model comes with a grill/griddle module and a two burner open-coil module. Either can be interchanged with a two burner cartridge. A wok can be plugged into an open coil burner, and a rectangular stew pot can replace the grill. In addition to a variety of cooking modules, Jenn-Air's six burner electric cooktop offers all four electric cooking options — conventional coil, solid element, glass-ceramic, or induction. The cooktop also includes a lift-up wood cutting board which covers a utensil storage compartment.

KitchenAid has a cutting board that fits into the griddle/grill area. Thermador's four burner convertible electric cooktop has a rotisserie unit for roasting turkeys and large cuts of meat.

General Electric's Monogram modular electric cooktop has interchangeable burners, grill, and griddle as well as downdraft ventilation and a fifth fixed Sensi-Temp™ solid element burner.

AEG Design Andi-Co, the United States importer of AEG appliances, has a modular cooktop system which lets you design your own cooktop with gas and electric units. You could line up a

Modern Maid's solid disk electric glass cooktop with removable grill or griddle. Photo courtesy of Modern Maid.

Broan's Eclipse downdraft ventilation system fits virtually any cooktop on the market. Photo courtesy of Broan.

Modern Maid's 36-inch gas cooktop with grill module that is dishwasher safe. Photo courtesy of Modern Maid.

module with two gas burners; followed by a down-draft ventilation unit; then a deep fryer; and another ventilation unit; then end up with a two-burner electric module. The deep fryer space is convertible to a griddle or grill, as are the other modules. There are covers for each of the modules. Gaggenau has a similar arrangement.

Jenn-Air and Modern Maid have a gas grill/griddle for their gas powered cooktops. The grill area can also be interchanged with a two burner module. KitchenAid manufactures a four burner gas cooktop with an area for an electric grill or fifth solid disk electric element which comes with a wood cover.

Most of the convertible cooktops are down-vented, thus eliminating the need for an overhead fan and hood. The ventilation systems have variable speeds, making grilling indoors feasible.

INDOOR GRILLS

If you live in a part of the country where outdoor grilling is not practical in the winter, you might want to consider a grill in your kitchen. There are two possibilities for an indoor grill. One is the grill module for a cooktop, as mentioned previously. The other is a separate grill unit installed in the counter.

The separate unit is usually a gas fired one which can be installed in your countertop or in a specially built area in the kitchen. Thermador makes a gas grill in two sizes — 19-inch or 29-inch width. When not in use, the Thermador Char-Glo grill can be covered with a stainless steel lid which provides additional counter space. Gaggenau has a grill and deep fryer in one unit with a powerful ventilation system.

The first separate electric grills were introduced by the Jenn-Air Company at the 1990 National Association of Home Builders Show in Atlanta. The two models offered are an 18-inch wide single grill and a 30-inch wide double one. Both feature the downdraft ventilation system that Jenn-Air pioneered with its electric grill cooktop mod-

ules. Under-counter drain jars collect drippings from the grilling food.

The Jenn-Air grill elements are permanently installed but are hinged to swing up to remove the grill rocks for cleaning and to wipe out the porcelainized steel grill basin. Recommended grill settings for the most commonly grilled foods are printed on the control panel.

Instead of a separate grill, another option for indoor grilling is a cartridge that can be plugged into a down-vented convertible electric or gas cooktop system, as previously mentioned. Most of these units are 10 inches wide. The down-vented fan removes any smoke and cooking odors. With some manufacturers the grill is part of the standard cooktop, with others it is an extra option. Jenn-Air, General Electric, Gaggenau, Dacor, Modern Maid, and KitchenAid all have grills for their electric cooktops as well as their gas ones. Gaggenau's electric grill has twelve temperature settings as does the one for General Electric.

Modern Maid's 36-inch gas cooktop has a Teflon coated grill module which is dishwasher safe. A grease jar is not needed since an easy to remove and clean grease pan fits under the porcelain grill module.

Some cooktop grills come with lava rocks while others have wrought-iron plates. The rocks or iron plates heat up along with the heating element. When cooking juices land on either, they sizzle and send smoke to the food which gives it the grilled taste. Both the rocks and iron plates work very well, but the plates are easier to clean. Lava rocks over time absorb grease and need to be cleaned periodically in hot soapy water.

Gaggenau's cooktop grill comes with rocks under the electric element. The unit has two separate elements, each with its own control to vary the heat for slow or fast grilling. Jenn-Air and General Electric have cooktop grills with bumpy iron plates that are easily removed for cleaning. Modern Maid has a gas cooktop with a grill similar to an outdoor gas grill with lava rocks above the burner and below the grill.

With all of these units a powerful ventilation system is a necessity, whether it is a variable speed downdraft system or a powerful overhead fan with hood.

EXHAUST FANS

As several writers have stated, the kitchen may be the "heart of the home" but it is also the center of air pollution. If the cooking area is not well ventilated, grease, smoke, odors, and moisture from cooking spread fast throughout the house. These unwanted odors, grease, and humid air can leave greasy coatings on walls and furniture, penetrate walls and insulation, and leave an uncomfortable atmosphere throughout the house.

This is particularly true in today's tightly constructed, energy efficient homes. With tighter insulation, thermo-pane windows, and fewer cracks around doors, there is almost no place for cooking fumes to seep through to the outdoors.

Kitchen ventilation is vital to the health and comfort of the home, and if there is an indoor grill adequate ventilation to the outside is essential. The most efficient place to dispose of the unwanted fumes is at the source — the kitchen range or cooktop. Capturing cooking fumes and ducting them to the outside with the help of a blower has proved to be the best way to ventilate.

There are two basic types of kitchen ventilation systems — downdraft and updraft. The former uses a fan to pull cooking fumes down from the range or built-in cooktop and through a vent pipe to the outside. The most common way to do this is to build a ventilation system into the range or cooktop with an air grille at the surface. A filter traps some of the grease and a duct carries the rest along with the odors to the outside of the house.

In the updraft system, a fan above the range pulls fumes up from the cooking surface. After passing through a filter they are ducted to the outside. There are also ventless range hood models that filter the air through a charcoal filter and then recirculate it in the kitchen. This system can remove some grease, smoke, and odors, but not steam and heat.

The size of the fan in a downdraft ventilation system is determined by the appliance manufacturer. The size of the fan in the updraft system depends on the type and location of the cooktop and the type of ductwork. The cooktop or range hood should extend three to six inches in length beyond the burners on each side for maximum efficiency.

The power of an exhaust fan is measured in CFM — cubic feet of air moved per minute. The farther the cooktop is from the vent the higher the CFM requirement. A standard downdraft cooktop should be vented with a 300 CFM fan. A good rule of thumb for a non-grill updraft cooktop in an island is to provide a minimum of 50 CFM per linear foot of range hood length. If a non-grill cooktop is installed against a wall it requires slightly less — a minimum of 40 CFM per linear foot of hood length. Commercial ranges which give off more heat require stronger fans, usually 600 CFM.

Downdraft ventilation systems have grown in popularity over the last decade. Most of these systems are built into the range or cooktop by the manufacturer. Broan Mfg. Co.'s "Eclipse" downdraft ventilation system fits virtually any cooktop on the market, and is sold independent of the cooktop. This means that virtually any cooktop can have a downdraft ventilation system. The Eclipse is a periscope vent that rises 7 inches above the cooktop by simply touching its cover. Touching a button lowers the unit flush to the countertop. The unit is easy to install and uses standard 6-inch duct work.

Hoods and fans can be purchased separately. Hoods come in a variety of materials such as stainless steel, copper, brass, enamel, and the wood cabinet type. When used over a center island, an attractive hood can become the focal point of the room.

Some of the hoods and fans available are from Best, USA, Inc. of Keamy, New Jersey, who make several models of hoods in white, brass, black, and several designer combinations. They also have a combination hood and fan that recirculates the air inside the kitchen through charcoal filters. Abbaka has custom designed range hoods suited for kitchens with gables or ceilings of more than 98 inches high. They can be either wall or ceiling mounted. Dacor makes a downdraft ventilation system for installation with cooktops which do not have this facility.

There is also a hideaway combination hood and fan made by Broan Mfg. Co., which resembles a cabinet when not in use. When the fan is needed, the frame of the cabinet is pulled out at the bottom, activating the fan. There is shallow storage space behind the hood's doors. Cabinet manufacturers can also provide the wall cabinet for such a ventilation system.

Some of the appliance manufacturers, such as Maytag, also produce separate range hoods with fans that fit above their ranges. The Maytag stainless steel hood is equipped with a variable speed fan and a three stage light.

General Electric has a wall-mounted microwave oven with a powerful two-speed fan and a flip-out tempered glass spatter shield. (See description under Microwave Ovens.)

Gaggenau produces an ultra-flat updraft ventilation system that is mounted under an overhead cabinet. The vapor screen can be pushed under the cabinet when not in use. The unit has three speeds and a flashing light on the control panel will remind you when it is time to clean the grease filter. The metal filter is easily pulled out and cleaned in the dishwasher. This kitchen hood also works on a winter-summer basis which means that in cold weather the hood does not work on an "air-output" basis but recirculates air through a charcoal filter. However, the unit can work either way.

Abbaka, a Danish manufacturer, has recently introduced its newest luxury hood design, the Module-Aire™. Consisting of four individual interconnecting sections, the modular construction of the hood allows one to mix or match decorative metal and colored finishes. This flexibility enhances the ability to integrate the hood into the overall design of the kitchen. For example, five different finishes ranging from polished brass, white enamel, satin finish stainless steel, copper, or matte black enamel, in addition to custom colors, can be used in the hood.

Available in both wall mount or free hanging island designs, standard sizes of the Module-Aire™ can accommodate ranges up to 48 inches in kitchens with up to 9 foot ceilings. The fan produces 600 or 1200 CFM. An accessory to hang cooking utensils from the hood is available.

CONVENTIONAL OVENS

Many ovens today have several modes of operation which combine two or even three energy uses — conventional heat (called radiant heat by the industry), convection heat, and microwaves. The only difference between conventional and convection heat is that the latter oven is equipped with an internal fan that circulates the hot air at high speed. All three cooking methods can be used in sequence or simultaneously in dual and triple energy ovens. Thermador's Convection MicroThermal oven has all three technologies in one unit.

However, combinations of two heat sources are the most commonly used. For example, you can use both microwaves and convection heat separately or simultaneously in one oven. The most popular combinations are radiant and convection, microwave and convection, or radiant and microwave. Modern Maid's Touch Tri-Mode Combination wall oven uses the latter combination in its upper oven. The cook has the option of using microwaves alone, conventional electric heat alone, or both simultaneously in the same oven. The upper oven also functions as a slow-cook, crockpot oven. It can also micro-broil which speeds up the broiling process yet leaves the meat very juicy. The lower oven has conventional heat and both are self-cleaning.

Self-Cleaning Ovens

Many of the ovens today are self-cleaning. They have a high temperature cleaning cycle which

KitchenAid's Superba™ built-in double oven features microwave-convection upper oven and a conventional radiant self-cleaning lower oven with two element balanced baking and roasting. Photo courtesy of KitchenAid.

Modern Maid's Touch Tri-Mode Combination Wall Oven with microwave and conventional electric heat in the upper oven. Both ovens are operated with an electronic keypad. Photo courtesy of Modern Maid.

burns spills into a white ash that can be easily wiped up. The cleaning takes about 2½ to 3½ hours. Most ovens have an automatic door-lock mechanism for the self-cleaning function. Continuous-cleaning ovens have interior surfaces that will dissolve most spills during the regular baking.

Although the self-cleaning feature is most desirable, these ovens have smaller interiors than those that do not have a self-cleaning feature. Since the oven has to be heated to about 800 degrees F. to burn off the accumulated stains, extra thick insulation has to be used to protect the surrounding walls and cabinets. This insulation takes up between 6 and 9 inches. The standard 27-inch self-cleaning ovens made by General Electric, Kitchen-Aid, and Modern Maid are 19 to 20 inches on the interior. Thus if you are buying a new oven take along the largest pan you use and see if it fits.

However, wider ovens are available, such as the 35-inch stainless-steel model from Gaggenau. Besides its additional width the oven has many other features. It has four heating systems — hot air, conventional radiant, hot air broil, and radiant broil. A rotisserie works with all of the heating systems. There are separate controls for top and bottom oven heating.

Automatic Oven Timers

Today's ovens can operate without the cook's presence. Delay/cook oven controls let you set a timer so that cooking will commence at a predetermined time. I like to use this feature to start dinner if I am away from the house when cooking should commence.

Electronic Controls for Ovens

Many of the ovens today feature electronic controls. If there is a double oven configuration then there are separate banks of function pads on the common control panel located above the upper oven. For instance, to program the electronic Jenn-Air double oven you simply touch the desired func-tion pad and turn the set dial to enter time or temperature. Indicator words in the display window flash to prompt the next step in programming, or to indicate an error. The display window also shows time and temperature simultaneously.

Electronic controls also allow the manufacturers to preset the oven thermostat and program the heat elements so that they will maintain more precise and even temperatures. The precise electronic programming of the self-cleaning cycle helps to minimize the odors normally associated with the process.

GAS OVENS

Built-in wall ovens are not limited to electric energy. In recent years, gas ovens have become available with many of the same features as the electric ovens, including self-cleaning. For example the self-cleaning, internally vented model from Modern Maid includes a patented Gourmet Broiler. This infrared broiler enables the cook to prepare restaurant quality steaks and chops in a minimum amount of time without preheating the oven. The Gourmet Broiler concentrates a consistent layer of infrared heating rays onto the food. This quickly sears the outside of the food, sealing in the natural juices. The unit also speeds up the broiling process by 35%.

Many of the broilers in the ovens are thermostatically controlled to adjust the broiling temperature, both in radiant and convection broiling.

Wall ovens are available in a variety of appliance colors as well as stainless steel. Black and white continue to be popular.

CONVECTION OVENS

Since the early 1950s, commercial bakeries and restaurants have been using convection ovens because more food can be placed in them and still achieve even baking. Restaurants also found that meats had an improved quality when cooked in a convection oven. In 1973, the first convection oven

Dacor's 30-inch Convection Plus oven, shown under a Dacor gas cooktop, bakes six tins of muffins at the same time. Photo courtesy of Dacor.

KitchenAid's combination microwave-convection oven with an exhaust unit is featured above a drop-in range. Photo courtesy of KitchenAid.

for home use, a countertop model, was produced in the United States. Today, many of the countertop model convection ovens are combined with a microwave capability and vice versa. Farberware is one of the few manufacturers still producing a countertop convection-only model. Convection cooking is an integral part of ranges and built-in wall ovens.

In a convection oven, a fan constantly recirculates hot air over the food at a high speed. The oven is similar to a radiant or conventional oven in that it has the same type of heating element, but the radiant oven does not use forced air. The moving hot air in a convection oven heats the surface of the food more rapidly, thus speeding up the cooking process. Using a convection oven instead of a radiant one decreases cooking time and saves energy.

A convection oven has many advantages, such as cooking meats faster so that they are juicer. Baked goods are lighter and more evenly textured. Foods also brown more evenly at lower temperatures. Since air circulates in the oven, three-rack baking is possible for large quantities of food. Preheating of the oven is rarely necessary. The fan alone can be used to dry foods or defrost frozen foods.

Dacor manufactures a 30-inch Convection Plus oven which is self cleaning. The oven has three 24-inch wide racks, which allow food on six cookie sheets to be baked at once. In addition to pure convection, the oven can also be programmed for standard bake, standard broil, convection bake, and convection broil. The Convection Plus oven control panel is symbolized for easy reading.

MICROWAVE OVENS

Microwave ovens use high-frequency radio waves to cook food without heating the air surrounding it. A magneton tube bombards food in a microwave oven and causes the food molecules to oscillate. This causes friction which creates heat within the food rather than the oven walls or the container, thereby providing faster and more efficient cooking.

Microwave ovens may be portable, built into an upper or lower cabinet, part of a wall oven unit, or part of a free-standing range. The microwave function can be combined with convection or radiant heating in one oven.

Many of the built-in microwave ovens units also contain an exhaust fan. These units can be part of an eye-level range, installed above a drop-in free-standing range, or be built in against a wall. General Electric pioneered this microwave oven concept in the late 1970s with its Spacesaver Unit. My General Electric microwave oven with 2-speed fan is installed above the preparation area where I frequently use an electric wok. The powerful fan eliminates odors and any grease created by wok cooking.

Microwave ovens make the best use of electronic controls. They program the oven to defrost and then cook at different heats. You can also program a pause to enable stirring the ingredients or changing the program while the food is cooking. Some microwave ovens have built-in recipe files which can recall and then cook by a certain sequence of steps, automatically.

Other features of microwave ovens include: a push-to-start control and end of cycle signal; a browning element; an automatic setting to defrost meat, poultry, or fish by weight; a temperature probe; and a memory feature that lets you program a series of cooking instructions and times. In some ovens, a sensor lets you know when the food is done.

Some cooks say that the combination of microwave and convection oven is an ideal way to cook. However, others say that if you use both methods of energy at the same time, the results are not as satisfactory as using one at a time. The combination seems to work best with "micro-roasting" poultry, which cooks the meat quickly so that it remains moist and also browns it. If space is limited, consider the combination that would give you both a microwave and a convection oven.

Microwave ovens are everywhere — the office, college dorms, summer homes, and hunting lodges. They have become accepted and in many instances indispensable. They have been accepted by the great cooks of the world. Traditional recipes are being adapted for the microwave and new ones are being created constantly. Their use is no longer limited to boiling water and heating coffee.

6
Cold Storage Appliances

Cold storage appliances have changed over the years. Not long ago there were only a few styles of separate refrigerators, separate freezers, and some combination refrigerators/freezers on the market. They all came in basic white and the refrigerator/freezer combinations were a single door unit with a freezer compartment inside the refrigerator. Today, there are many models of refrigerator/freezers, including both free-standing and built-in units. These models perform more functions and are better looking than they were ten years ago. Although freezers are included in most units, the term for this cold storage appliance has been shortened to refrigerators.

Studies have shown that most people purchase a new refrigerator about every fifteen years. In a period of fifteen years, lifestyles change, the family increases or decreases, and cooking and eating habits change. With that in mind, it is a good idea to assess your present and possible future cold storage needs before purchasing a refrigerator.

The advent and widespread use of takeout food has lessened the need for a separate freezer or a large refrigerator in the average kitchen. If you eat out frequently and shop every day or so, you will not want as large a refrigerator as the person who cooks every meal and grocery shops once a week.

The cook who grocery shops frequently and likes to prepare fresh food will want less freezer space than the person who shops every two or three weeks and uses the freezer for food storage. A family with children who frequently prepare sandwiches or snacks will want a refrigerator unit with a special storage tray for luncheon meats and cheeses. Those who use ice cubes often will want an icemaker in the freezer compartment as well as an in-the-door ice dispenser.

Also to be taken into consideration when planning refrigerator storage space is the type and frequency of entertaining. If you cook ahead for special occasions and freeze the food, you will want a large capacity freezer as well as refrigerator.

Since we like fresh fruits and vegetables, I need more space in the summer for storage of fresh produce and consequently like a large refrigerator. Melons, for instance, take up a great deal of space. For fresh seasonal produce and for storing foods prepared ahead for entertaining, I have an additional refrigerator and a freezer in the basement.

Experts recommend 12 cubic feet of refrigerator storage space for the first two family members and 2 more additional cubic feet for each additional member. Refrigerators come in all sizes from small bar refrigerators that have only a few cubic feet of storage space to 30-plus cubic foot units that offer numerous types of shelving, containers, and convenience options. Manufacturers' research has shown that models of about 17 cubic feet are the most popular with the average four person household, with 22 cubic feet being ideal.

When purchasing a new refrigerator it is a good idea to be sure it will fit into the space designated for it. Since on some units the door is reversible, you should consider whether you need a right or left hand door opening. This is assuming that you are not purchasing a side-by-side refrigerator/freezer. You should have at least 12 inches of counter space beside the door opening to put down items going into the refrigerator or coming out of it.

TYPES OF REFRIGERATORS

There is a wide choice of refrigerator models. You can select from single door, two door, three door, and multiple door and drawer units. The freezer can be located at the top or bottom, or in a side-by-side unit. The single door unit, popular many years ago, is still available with a small freezer compartment inside. Since the door is opened every time such a unit is used, the freezer is not as efficient as one with a separate door.

In overall national sales, the top-mount (top-freezer) unit is the most popular. The top-mount refrigerators with the freezer on top have two wide doors, one for the freezer and one for the refrigerator. These doors require a generous clearance space for the swing of the doors, both in front of, and adjacent to, the unit. A possible disadvantage to the top-mount refrigerator is that in this type of unit the freezer is not easily accessible to children.

Bottom-mount models, as the name suggests, have the freezer on the bottom, either with a separate door or with a pull-out drawer. The bottom-mount model of refrigerator is also available with French doors (2 doors for the refrigerator) and a pull out drawer for the freezer. This type of unit has a large, wide refrigerator compartment and a chest-type freezer.

The side-by-side refrigerator, just as the name implies, has two doors side by side, one for the refrigerator and one for the freezer. Side-by-side models have the advantage of having most of the food within easy sight and reach, if not at eye or shoulder level. The side-by-side unit generally has a more deluxe appearance, more features, more organized storage, and needs less door clearance. Also if you are short or tall you do not have to stretch or bend as much to reach the food. One

complaint, however, of the side-by-side units is that the shelves are too narrow and make food storage difficult. I have a side-by-side unit and have had no trouble placing large casseroles and soufflé dishes on the shelves.

Traulsen, a company that pioneered the development of top-mounted refrigeration systems (the mechanism), self-closing doors, and digital temperature monitoring systems, today makes commercial-quality refrigerators. The units vary in width from 36 to 48 inches and are 24 inches deep for a built-in look, although they are free-standing.

Many of the Traulsen refrigerators have bins at the bottom to keep frequently used items within easy reach without opening the refrigerator door. These bins contain anodized aluminum pans that are ideal for storing fresh fish and poultry covered with ice. The Traulsen unit includes an icemaker that dispenses up to fifteen pounds of ice into an external drawer. Traulsen also produces a 48-inch stand-alone refrigerator for the person who entertains extensively and wants ample cold storage space.

FEATURES OF REFRIGERATORS

Manufacturers of today's refrigerators are very energy conscious, as evidenced by the information sticker on each unit in your dealer's showroom. This sticker has information about the amount of yearly energy used by the appliance and the approximate cost of its operation.

The compressor in the refrigerator is responsible for circulating Freon®, the cooling agent which removes heat from the refrigerator. The operation of the compressor should be smooth and quiet and should also have a high-reserve cooling capacity. This means that both the refrigerator and freezer will be kept at their designated temperatures in extremely hot weather.

There is increased cooling flexibility in today's refrigerators. For instance, Amana units have thermostatically controlled dampers that direct the cold air to where it is needed the most. For proper

Traulsen's 36-inch refrigerator/freezer with see-through tempered glass refrigerator doors. Photo courtesy of Traulsen.

Traulsen's refrigerator/freezer with tempered glass doors. Photo courtesy of Traulsen.

Traulsen's Ultra 48-inch refrigerator/freezer with automatic icemaker. Photo courtesy of Traulsen.

food storage the refrigerator compartment should be about 37 degrees F. and the freezer at 0 degrees F. The coldness of the milk and the firmness of the ice cream are good ways to judge the temperature of the units.

Most refrigerators have separate temperature controls for the refrigerator and freezer. All of Sub-Zero's refrigerator/freezers have two compressors which provide independent control for the freezer and refrigerator compartments. This independent functioning of each unit makes for greater efficiency. Many refrigerators, such as Whirlpool's DesignerStyle™, have the temperature controls in or near the front of the unit.

Defrosting a refrigerator is almost passé. Refrigerators are available in automatic defrost and partial defrost models. The latter, also known as cycle defrost, defrosts the cooling section in the refrigerator each time the unit stops running, but the freezer section must be defrosted manually. Whirlpool's defrost mechanism monitors operating conditions to determine when to defrost.

Some refrigerators have thermometers that monitor room temperature and humidity. For example, General Electric cycles warm refrigerant around the front of the freezer to prevent condensation from forming on the exterior of the unit. Traulsen refrigerators have a defogger control which prevents condensation from forming on the cabinet exterior by activating concealed heating wires. This is necessary since most of the Traulsen refrigerator exteriors are stainless steel, and some have tempered glass doors.

There are many handy features in today's refrigerators. An automatic icemaker is almost a must if you like cold drinks and they are a standard feature on many units. The automatic icemaker does require a separate water supply which comes through a small tube at the back of the unit. Before purchasing such a refrigerator, make sure that this water supply can be provided in your kitchen. Many side-by-side units have an in-the-door dispenser for both ice and chilled water, so that you can get either without opening the freezer door.

There is also a control which gives you either ice cubes, squares or crescents, or crushed ice.

Another cold option is offered by Jenn-Air, Admiral, and Magic Chef. Their deluxe units offer an optional automatic ice-cream maker.

The deluxe models from the major refrigerator manufacturers have electronic programming that regulate temperature of the fresh-food and freezer compartments, defrost when necessary, monitor and correct crisper and meat storage temperatures, and monitor the operating system for potential problems. The electronic panel may also include an alarm which sounds when the door is left open. Thanks to the microchip, the display panel can also warn you of operational problems. Traulsen refrigerators have a digital readout which gives you the exact refrigerator or freezer temperature at the flick of a switch.

There are a variety of colors available in refrigerators, with almond being the most popular, followed by light gray. White is making a great comeback and black is being increasingly used as an accent color. Many manufacturers offer wood or laminate insert panels for the front and sides of the refrigerator to coordinate with your kitchen cabinets. If the manufacturer does not have the panels to match he can provide the necessary hardware for installing your own matching cabinet panels, which are available from the cabinet manufacturers.

STORAGE

There are about as many shelving options as there are models of refrigerators from which to choose. Some of the basic models still have fixed wire shelving, but most of the more deluxe units have tempered glass shelves for easy cleaning. Most of the shelves are adjustable up or down to provide flexibility in storing items of different size. Whirlpool's DesignerStyle™ refrigerator has adjustable Spillguard™ tempered glass shelves which slide out and have raised edges to contain up to twelve ounces of spilled liquid.

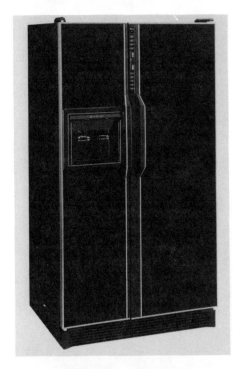

Amana's new side-by-side refrigerator/ freezer features a black textured steel cabinet with matching black handles and polycarbonate door panels. Photo courtesy of Amana.

Some of the refrigerators have half shelves which can be adjusted to provide a space of greater height in part of the refrigerator. Gibson refrigerators have a patented 4-in-One shelf that is a partial shelf. It can be used as a wine rack, a can dispenser, turned over and used as a flat shelf, or it can be removed entirely so that tall items can be stored. Wine chilling racks that hold two bottles are an optional accessory, featured by Jenn-Air and Admiral.

Refrigerator and freezer doors offer very accessible and frequently-used storage space. In most models both the refrigerator and freezer doors are equipped with a variety of bins and shelves. In the refrigerator, there is egg storage with removable trays and see-through covered butter and cheese compartments that help retain flavor and freshness. Shelves or bins with retaining bars are designed for large containers or bottles, such as half gallon milk containers and two liter bottles.

Many of the refrigerator and freezer door shelves and bins are adjustable. General Electric has moveable "keepers" in its door bins. These "keepers" are dividers that can be placed against an item to keep it from falling over or to divide the bin. This is particularly helpful when the shelf is not completely full. I have made a small compartment with one of my door "keepers" and store lemons or limes in it.

Special drawers in the refrigerator provide proper storage for fruits, vegetables, meats, and snack food such as cheese and luncheon meats. Meat drawers usually have their own temperature controls so that the meat will retain its freshness longer. The colder temperature in the meat drawer comes directly from the cold air in the freezer. The temperature control on the meat drawer regulates this air flow. Thus meat can be kept several degrees cooler than the temperature in the rest of the refrigerator.

Crisper drawers are used to store fruits and vegetables. They should be large enough to hold a head of lettuce or cauliflower and even a large melon. Many of the crispers have their own thermostats and some refrigerators also have moist crispers which provide a humidity control that can be adjusted for high or low level humidity. Maintaining proper humidity can lengthen the life of lettuce and leafy vegetables.

Some refrigerators have other conveniences. For example, the General Electric Monogram Side-by-Side unit has two large and three small covered snack trays which are microwavable. These trays are stored in a rack under one of the upper shelves of the refrigerator. You can store food in the covered trays and then heat them up in the microwave. General Electric's Spacecenter unit has a door-in-a-door, which provides access to frequently used items without opening the main refrigerator door.

Freezers, too, have adjustable shelves and many also have pull-out wire trays for easy retrieval of bulky items. Even in most side-by-side units, the freezers have shelves deep enough to store large casseroles. The Whirlpool DesignerStyle™ freezer section has a quick freeze compartment and an adjustable pizza rack to hold several frozen pizzas, up to 13 inches in diameter.

The Sub-Zero side-by-side refrigerator/freezers have multiple roll-out baskets in the freezers for easy access. There are also four roll-out crispers in the refrigerator section, as well as a tray for snack storage.

BUILT-IN REFRIGERATORS

With the great interest in sleek, uncluttered kitchen designs, the need has developed to reduce the depth of refrigerators. A free-standing refrigerator protrudes into the room 4 to 6 inches beyond the cabinets, creating an awkward appearance and taking up valuable space in the kitchen. With shallower refrigerators, the width of kitchen aisles can be increased. There is another advantage to the shallower depth of the built-in refrigerator. The shallower shelves make it easier to find what you are looking for and eliminate the need to search for items which have found their way to the back of the shelves.

Sub-Zero was the industry leader in 24-inch deep refrigerators that fit flush with standard kitchen counters. Today most manufacturers produce built-in as well as free-standing 24-inch refrigerators. These units are all the same depth, but vary in width as well as height. Many models have decorative panels which can be applied to coordinate with cabinets.

In order to provide more cubic feet of storage space most of the built-in refrigerators are 36 or 42 inches wide. They come in either side-by-side configurations or with the refrigerator on top and the freezer on the bottom. Also available are separate 36-inch refrigerators and freezers which can be placed side by side for a coordinated appearance.

KitchenAid's built-in 84-inch high refrigerator with top-mounted refrigeration system. Photo courtesy of KitchenAid.

Some manufacturers, such as KitchenAid, have added extra height to their 24-inch deep built-ins in order to provide more storage space. The unit has a top-mounted refrigeration system that can be serviced from the front. The refrigerator can be installed in place of a conventional refrigerator by removing any existing overhead cabinet. General Electric's Monogram series also has a 24-inch built-in refrigerator. It is 42 inches wide and can accommodate full size trays in the refrigerator section. This General Electric built-in unit also has the refrigeration system on top.

For its 24-inch built-in refrigerator, Modern Maid has available optional white overhead cabinet doors, enabling the homeowner to build a cabinet on top of the refrigerator flush with the front of the unit. This provides extra storage space, but gives the appearance of an extra large refrigerator.

Many refrigeration units are now designed to blend with any kitchen decor. This is made possible through the use of removable decorative panels, either wood or laminate, which match the kitchen cabinets and can be changed with the decor of the cabinets. The optional panels can be installed on the front as well as the sides of the refrigerators. Many units, such as Sub-Zero, are designed with a minimum of external hardware so that the units blend into the kitchen decor. The exterior of the Sub-Zero model 561 is designed so that ¼-inch thick decorative panels can be installed. Colored and stainless steel panels are available from the factory.

OTHER COLD STORAGE APPLIANCES

Gone are the days when you had to decide if you wanted a freezer and where you wanted to place it. Although freezers are now part of the refrigerator, free-standing freezer units are still available for those who freeze a great amount of food. Freezers are available in upright and chest type models. The former have shelves and pull-out bins, while the latter have removable trays and bins.

Under-the-counter refrigerators are popular in the hospitality area of the kitchen for beverage storage and prepared hors d'oeuvre trays. The under-the-counter models range in capacity from 2.9 cubic feet to about 4.4 cubic feet and in width from 17 to 36 inches. These units are standard counter height and depth. They are well insulated and many are available with decorative front panels. Some of the units have a small freezer compartment for ice cubes; others are simply total refrigerators. There are also under-the-counter freezer units.

Built-in under-the-counter icemakers are also available for those who entertain frequently. Sub-

Traulsen's under-the-counter refrigerator. Photo courtesy of Traulsen.

Zero makes an icemaker that is only 12 inches wide, has an "easy-tilt" door, and an automatic shut-off so that it makes ice only as you use it. Other units are either 18 or 24 inches wide and can be obtained with decorative panels. KitchenAid's Architectural Series automatic icemaker produces up to 51 pounds of ice daily. Its lighted bin holds 35 pounds and refills automatically when the ice supply runs low.

To maintain wine at an ideal temperature, Traulsen produces several wine refrigerators which maintain a consistent temperature range of 53 to 57 degrees F. There is an exterior digital read-out which tells you the exact interior temperature of the unit. Specially designed adjustable wine racks hold the bottles in a tilted position to keep the corks moist. These wine racks are also available for

*Wine refrigerator by Traulsen maintains a
consistent temperature suitable for wine
storage and has specially designed
adjustable racks. Photo courtesy of
Traulsen.*

Traulsen's under-counter refrigeration unit. Jenn-
Air also produces a special refrigerator to store
forty bottles of wine at wine cellar temperature.

7
Sinks and Cleanup Appliances

The sink area is one that gets constant use. The cleanup area of the kitchen used to be centered around a cast iron or a white enamel sink, with a drainboard attached. Today the cleanup center of the kitchen contains not only a sink but appliances such as a dishwasher, disposal, and trash compactor — all of which have made washing dishes and cleaning up easier and speedier.

The past fifty years have seen the old, ugly kitchen sink gradually transformed into a thing of beauty. Today kitchen sinks are available in a brilliant array of colors and a variety of materials. There are also many configurations and designs of sinks as well as accessories to make your cleanup chores easier. Faucets, too, have become updated and offer a variety of options.

Since dishwashing is an unpleasant but necessary chore, sinks were traditionally placed along a wall under a window. Today many sinks are still located under a window, but also a great number are installed in an island or peninsula with a view out into the kitchen or the family room. These placements offer the "dishwasher" distractions such as a view of the garden, the television, or conversation with the family in the adjacent family room. Placing the sink across a corner in the kitchen will enlarge the kitchen counter space, but usually eliminates a view.

The sink is primarily used for cleanup, to fill pots and pans with water for cooking, and to prepare fruits, vegetables, and other foods. If there are two cooks in the family, you might want an additional, specially designed food preparation sink which could also be used as a bar sink. Many of the bar sinks, unfortunately, are too small to use as food preparation sinks.

Sinks are made of three basic materials: stainless steel, enameled cast iron, and man-made materials such as bonded quartz and glass-reinforced polyester. Except for stainless steel, many sinks have a textured finish on the bottom to prevent pots and pans from skidding. Again, except for stainless steel, sinks are available in a wide variety of colors from soft pastels and versatile earth tones to eye-catching bright colors as well as black and white.

The difference between an enameled cast-iron sink and a stainless steel one is basically a matter of decor. Both are durable, although stainless steel is virtually indestructible and enamel can chip on rare occasions However, enamel coatings have been greatly improved in the last decade. As far as price is concerned, the best quality of enameled cast iron sinks are about 20% more than the heavy 18-gauge stainless steel ones. The modern double-fired enamel sink will show few scratches and does not require the frequent scrubbing which was necessary with older enamel sinks. Heavy-gauge stainless is virtually carefree and scratches, unless they are very deep ones, are not noticeable.

Stainless steel sinks are available in two thicknesses, 18 and 20 gauge. The 20 gauge sink is thicker and therefore is likely to last longer. The metal of both gauges contains some chromium and nickel to resist staining and corrosion. Stainless steel sinks also do not fade, chip, and crack. Many

Kohler's Julienne™ hexagonal sink with smaller disposal basin and built in small drainboards. Photo courtesy of Kohler Co.

Kohler's Entertainer™ sink used as a double corner sink. Cutting board and strainers make left-hand sink suitable for bood preparation.

of the manufacturers have a finish on their stainless steel sinks which prevents scratching, such as El-kay's Lasting Beauty™. Kohler's stainless steel sinks are undercoated with a special sound absorbing material called Hushcoat to reduce noise and disposal vibration.

The Kohler Company is one of the largest manufacturers of enameled cast iron sinks and The El-kay Manufacturing Company has one of the largest lines of stainless steel sinks.

The glass-reinforced polyester sink is strong, durable, and exceptionally resistant to heat and high temperatures. It also resists cracking, staining, and discoloring. Since the glass-reinforced polyester sink has a smooth, nonporous finish, it is easy to care for and can be wiped clean with a soft cloth and gentle cleanser.

Sink sizes vary greatly and sink units are available in single, double, or triple configurations, with or without attached drainboards. Although the standard size of a kitchen sink is 33 by 22 inches, most manufacturers offer sizes that range from 16 by 19 inches to 43 by 22 inches. The depths of these sinks vary from 6½ inches to 10 inches. The disposal basins (also known as small sinks) attached to

larger sinks are 2 to 5 inches in depth.

The diversity in sizes is matched by an assortment of available shapes, including the traditional rectangular and square basins, as well as new and innovative round, kidney-shaped, and crescent-shaped designs. Sink designers have updated the square and rectangular shapes with the European styling of rounded corners. Franke's new Sunline™ sink, created by world-renowned designer Luigi Colani, has an extraordinary sculpted form. The technique used to create this sink is a new one.

The square sink is the basis of many sink configurations and can be space efficient in a small kitchen. Many of the square sinks come with bowls that are rounded in the back for a contemporary look and for practicality since more large pots and pans fit into that type of sink. The square sink can have a smaller preparation or disposal sink attached to it. The same is true for a rectangular sink, which can either have one large rectangular unit with a smaller one attached or two rectangular sinks with a even smaller sink in the middle. Whichever configuration you choose, be sure to specify which sink you want on the left or right.

In sink configurations there are high and low

sinks. A typical combination might have a 17″ × 17″ × 10″ square sink and a 9″ × 15″ × 6″ smaller sink. The former is deep enough to accommodate large cooking utensils and the latter's smaller basin is efficient for food preparation. A disposal is often installed in the smaller sink.

European styled sinks have the drain in the back, not the center, so that shelves can be installed in the space below the sink. However, if you are attaching a disposal to the drain of this sink there is no room for a shelf. Dishwasher connections will also interfere with an extra shelf. The European sink does not have a 4-inch wide rim in the back for the faucet because the faucet is typically placed in the corner of the sink flange. This permits the size of the bowl to be increased by about 10%.

Design is the focal point in the Kohler Julienne™ large enameled cast iron sink. It combines a hexagonal basin with a small triangular one. Although unusually shaped, the large basin measures 29 inches side to side and 16½ inches front to back. Located in the upper left hand corner of the Julienne is a small basin which serves primarily as a disposal compartment. A drain board is in the upper right hand corner of the sink. A wooden cutting board, designed to cover half of the basin, converts the sink into a food preparation center.

The new "Connoisseur" sink from American Standard has rounded bowls with a straight back. The sink is suitable for corner and standard countertop installations.

You can also custom design a sink unit to fit your individual needs. It is possible to mix and match bowl components with Vance Industries' Epure collection of sculptured stainless steel shapes. For instance, you can create a three bowl sink by using two kidney shape bowls with a round bowl in the center. Also available from Vance Industries are uniquely designed single and double bowl sinks in their American series. The International series is available with attached ribbed drainboards.

The two-cook family has created the need for an additional preparation sink. Although two people may cook together, it is difficult to share a sink when both are preparing food. The solution in some kitchens has been to install a bar sink. However, this is not an ideal solution because the bar sink has an undersized bowl, is frequently rectangular, and is awkward to use. Most of the bar sinks only have a 2-inch drain which eliminates the use of a disposal.

The new small European designed round sinks, such as those manufactured by Abbaka, have become an excellent solution for a second preparation sink. They have a deep bowl, large drain, and useful accessories such as a fitted chopping board and drainer baskets. Often the absence of a faucet ledge on this type of "prep sink," combined with its round shape, allows for the installation of a versatile faucet as well as other sink accessories. This "prep sink" can also be used as the bar or hospitality sink.

Hospitality sinks can be square or round and measure between 16 and 20 inches in width or diameter. The hospitality sink can be installed in the bar area or on an island in the kitchen away from the work traffic of the kitchen. These sinks can be brass, stainless steel, a combination of brass and stainless, enameled cast iron, or a composition material. Kohler's Porto Fino™ enameled cast iron round sink is self rimmed, and has a flat bottom with a ⅝-inch drain, a standard requirement for disposals. This sink can also be used as a corner placement since it has a counter-mounted faucet feature.

One of the most versatile hospitality sinks is Kohler's enameled cast iron Entertainer™ — a crescent shape sink which has a 22 by 18 inch basin. It can be used in the hospitality center or as a second sink in the kitchen. When two of the sinks are installed side by side they become a two-basin kitchen sink with a unique design and are especially suitable for a corner installation.

Sinks can be installed in the kitchen either on top of the counter, mounted flush with the counter, or recessed underneath the counter. If mounted on top the sinks have a rim of the same material as the

Kohler's enameled cast iron Entertainer™ which can be used as a hospitality sink or as a sink in a small kitchen. Photo courtesy of Kohler Co.

Kohler's Porto Fino™ round enameled cast iron sink can be used on an island in the hospitality area or as a corner placement. Photo courtesy of Kohler Co.

Kohler's Lakefield™ is especially designed for a flush installation with ceramic tile countertops for a clean, custom look.

sink. Flush-mounted models have a flat rim so that the sink can be installed flush with a tile countertop. This gives a neat and custom appearance, and is easier to maintain. The under-the-counter sinks are installed beneath pre-cut holes in the countertop with a lip of the counter material framing the sink. This type of installation is most often used with granite, marble, or man-made solid surfaces such as Corian™.

Undermounted sinks give a very sleek modern appearance to the kitchen and make the countertop area around them easy to maintain. Several manufacturers make this type of sink including Franke, Inc., at the moment the only producer of stainless steel sinks that mount under the counter. One or more sinks can be mounted this way to provide a double sink in the kitchen.

Kohler has combined a stainless steel sink with a cast composite material deck for long life and durability. The Silicast™ deck forms the rim and back shelf of the sink and is securely bonded to it. The deck, which provides a color accent as well as an easy-to-maintain surface, comes in white, almond, blue, teal, black, rose, cream, and gray to coordinate with a wide variety of kitchen decors.

SINK ACCESSORIES

Today the sink is not only the place to cleanup cooking utensils, rinse and wash dishes, but with the availability of accessories, the sink has become an adjunct to the food preparation center. You can now chop, slice, and rinse your vegetables without taking additional steps between the preparation area and the sink.

Hardwood cutting boards to fit either the smaller sink in a multiple sink configuration or to partially cover the main sink are available from virtually every sink manufacturer. Colanders are available that fit into the small sink, which are perfect for rinsing vegetables or collecting food scraps for disposal.

Colored vinyl-covered wire rinse baskets of var-ious sizes that fit sinks or attached drainboards are also available and make handy dish drainers. Some manufacturers, such as Elkay, offer a drain tray, which not only extends the work surface but is also ideal for rinsing and drying dishes. Many sinks are available with drainboards extended from the sink.

To pamper your hands, manufacturers offer both liquid dishwashing soap and lotion dispensers that can be installed beside the sink faucets. They are available in chrome, gold, brass, and decorator colors.

Bar sinks have their own accessory packages to turn the bar sink into a workable bar. The package usually contains a cutting board that fits over all or part of the sink. The cutting board has a hole in it to enable the faucet to be used. There are also containers for olives, cherries, or lemon slices in these bar accessory kits.

FAUCETS

There have been revolutionary changes in kitchen faucets in the last decade. Today there is a much wider choice in the type and design of faucets for the kitchen sink. Before the designers exerted their skills on kitchen faucets, the most common ones had a chrome finish and either chrome, porcelain, or glass handles.

European kitchen designs influenced American manufacturers to produce colored faucets, sculptured faucets, and faucets with retractable spray hoses.

Kitchen sink faucets are available in chrome, brass, and a variety of colors with either a single lever or two handles. The colored faucets are available in either acrylic or ceramic. There are also inserts of acrylic, wood, stone, crystal, and ceramic to provide a combination of colors and textures for faucets.

Various options for kitchen faucets include spout styles which may be stationary or swivel. The faucet may have a pull-out spout head or aerator attachment. European style single-lever faucets rotate front to back for temperature and rock left to

Grohe's Ladylux faucet with brush spray cleans fine china and crystal. Photo courtesy of Grohe.

right for flow rate. The single lever faucet is easier to operate since it controls temperature and volume in one operation.

In 1985 Grohe, a German manufacturer, introduced a new concept in kitchen faucets — a kitchen faucet with a pull-out spray head. Grohe's Ladylux faucet has this type of spray head which features two water patterns (steady flow and spray) and is interchangeable with other attachments such as a brush spray, scraper spray, or water filter head. The filter head is useful if you sometimes encounter grit in your water system. The Dual-Pattern Head, which has two spray systems, detaches with a single click. The Brush Spray gently cleans fine china and crystal and the Scraper Spray is ideal for dirty pots and pans.

Today many faucets are available with a pull-out retractable spray and hose which provide either a spray or an aerated water flow. Some sprayers such as Franke's models extend to two feet.

Although a high-arc faucet is usually installed with a bar sink, it is also desirable for the main kitchen sink if you wash many large items, such as stock pots and large pitchers. A taller arched faucet gives more flexibility to the sink since it can easily swing out of the way. In selecting a kitchen sink faucet you should also consider whether the faucet is going to be used with one or two sinks. If the latter is the case, you will want one with an extended reach or with a pull-out spray for the preparation sink.

Faucets can be mounted either directly on the sink or on the countertop. The latter is always used with an under counter-mounted sink. If two or more sinks are used as an under counter-mounted unit, the faucet is usually mounted between the sinks. Some faucets use a deck (an oblong piece of metal like the faucet) for the mounting between the sink and the faucet.

The valve is the most important working part of the faucet since it controls the flow of water. Elkay uses a Hi'n'Dry™ cartridge on many of their faucets. This cartridge uses a special rubber diaphragm instead of conventional washers. Many of Kohler's faucets have a wear-resistant, washerless ceramic cartridge. Abbaka uses two ceramic surfaces which rotate against each other to open and close the water passage. Franke's cartridge has an internal flow and temperature restrictor.

An electronic digital faucet is available with a time and water-temperature display that is solar powered by any incandescent light. It is called Vision and is manufactured by U. S. Brass.

Hot Water Dispensers

As life-styles become more demanding and rushed, people are searching for easier and quicker ways to complete daily household tasks. A new timesaving device is the hot water dispenser.

A hot water dispenser provides hot water instantly for making hot drinks, soups, and gelatins. It also speeds up the preparation of pastas, rice, and potatoes. You no longer have to wait for water to boil on the stove or in the microwave. With just

Broan's RedyHot™ hot water dispenser with gooseneck for filling mugs and large containers. Photo courtesy of Broan.

a push of a lever or a turn of a cap, depending on the model, you can instantly have hot water of nearly 200 degrees F. Typically, hot water dispensers are thermostatically controlled between 140 degrees F. and 190 degrees F.

Most of the hot water dispensers have a capacity of sixty cups of hot water per hour. For example, Broan's RedyHot® model dispenses hot water when the user presses the red fingertip push/pull lever. On this model a special on/off switch is attached to the 1000 watt main heater beneath the sink, allowing you to turn the unit off if you leave home for an extended period.

The instant hot water dispenser will tend to keep the area under the sink quite warm. I have found it an excellent place for raising yeast dough.

FOOD WASTE DISPOSERS

Food waste disposers are installed in the drain of the kitchen sink and are designed to dispose of food waste quickly and easily. Today's food waste disposers handle any type of soft, moist food waste. Hard foods such as bones or crab, oyster, clam, and lobster shells should not be put down the disposal, although KitchenAid advertises that bones and nuts shells can be ground in their disposers.

Garbage disposers are of two types — batch feed and continuous feed. As their name implies, the former is slower operating and must be fed in batches. In many models the lid locks the food into the grinding chamber and turns the machine on. Other models also have the lid, but use a separate electric switch to turn on the disposal.

When purchasing a garbage disposer select one with a sturdy motor, at least ½ horsepower. It should also be insulated against noise and have an anti-jam mechanism.

Most disposers have a manual reset overload protector, if the unit jams during operation. I found that button very handy when I accidentally put in something that was very hard and could not be ground easily, such as an oyster or crab shell. Some of the garbage disposers have an anti-jam reversing action which reverses the blades to free them.

The food grinding chamber should be made of a noncorrosive material. For example, KitchenAid's disposer has a food grinding chamber made of stainless steel with two 360 degree swivel impellers, while Frigidaire's grinding chamber is heavy gauge aluminum. Most models have sound insulation for quieter operation.

DISHWASHERS

The first generation of dishwashers was not as sophisticated as they are today. Dishes had to be scraped and rinsed before being put into the dishwasher. Many people complained that it was almost as much work as washing the dishes by hand.

Dishwashers clean dishes by sending whirling torrents of hot water into every nook and corner of the dishwasher. Depending on the model, there are either one, two, or three water spray arms in the dishwasher. The water is constantly being filtered through a screen to remove particles of food and soil and then this clean filtered water continues to cascade over the dishes. It is this continuous filtering of water combined with detergent, and several rinses, that results in sparkling clean dishes and glassware. Although the filters never need cleaning, many dishwashers have little plastic grates that trap large food particles, which can then be removed. Many dishwashers have a soft food disposer built into them.

Most dishwashers are constructed of steel, with insulated walls to hold the heat, and also to hold noise to a minimum. The interiors may be stainless steel, plastic, porcelain, or enameled steel. The racks in the dishwasher are either nylon or vinyl coated stainless steel and many models have adjustable racks with folding dividers, as well as a basket for silverware.

Today dishwashers are sophisticated appliances. They are better insulated, for quieter operation and heat retention. Dishwashers now have variable cycles, from rinse and hold to a selection of wash cycles which includes a heavy duty cycle for pots and pans; a light or gentle washing cycle for good china and crystal; and a normal cycle for everyday dishes with average soil. The rinse and hold cycle enables dishes to be placed in the dishwasher, rinsed, and held until a full load has been assembled. To save energy many dishwashers also have a non-heated drying cycle.

Some dishwasher models have an adjustable water pressure feature and/or an automatic water softener to further enhance the cleaning abilities of each cycle. Tappan, Kenmore, and Thermador have two or three different water levels for various dishwashing tasks.

The control panels for dishwashers are available with push buttons, dials, or computerized touch controls. Some of the deluxe models have digital display panels which monitor water temperature, water pressure, and time remaining in the current cycle. For example, General Electric's Monogram dishwasher has an electronic control system with digital readouts that tell you which cycle is operating or how much energy is being consumed. Audible signals on this model alert you to any potential problems.

Whirlpool's new all-white European-styled dishwasher has recessed controls, sixteen cycle and option combinations, in addition to quiet washing and delayed start. Photo courtesy of Whirlpool.

The cancel function on some dishwasher models is a desirable feature. This feature will cancel the cycle and drain the washtub immediately — a handy feature if a problem should occur.

Another feature built into some of the deluxe models is a delay-start option. This will allow you to program the dishwasher to start at a pre-assigned time, such as after the guests have returned to the living room and are not within hearing distance of the dishwasher. For example, Whirlpool has a six-hour delay wash on some of their models.

Some dishwashers preheat the water before the unit starts washing. Depending on the cycle, the water may be heated to 120 degrees F. or 140 degrees F. This is an energy saving feature since it allows you to set your water heater at a lower temperature than is normally needed for a dishwasher.

Most manufacturers have added a "quiet" feature to many of their dishwashers. The operating noise and resonance are reduced by extra layers of sound-absorbing insulation. The use of rubber housing and slower pump speeds helps to muffle the draining sounds. KitchenAid has a "Whisper Quiet" system on its Superba line, Whirlpool has a "Quiet Wash" system, General Electric has heavy sound insulation on its Monarch line, and Thermador has added "Hush Coat" insulation to some models. Although the machines are less noisy, the location and surrounding materials also affect the noise level of dishwashers.

In most kitchens, the dishwasher is built into the base cabinets to the right or the left of the sink. It is recommended that the dishwasher be located on the opposite side of your favored hand. If you are right-handed the dishwasher should be on the left hand side of the sink.

There are several dishwashers specifically designed for small kitchens. General Electric offers two models which can be installed under the sink, both measuring 34¼ inches high, 24 inches deep, and 24 inches wide. However, these dishwasher require a sink only 6 inches deep. Because the dishwasher is under the sink, the sinks are not suited to a waste food disposer. Frigidaire has an 18-inch under the counter model that has four cycles.

Portable dishwashers are also still available for small kitchens. Some of the front-loading models can be converted to a built-in at a later date. Although portable dishwashers may provide another work surface in the kitchen, many people complain that they are hard to move about and cumbersome to hook up to a sink faucet.

TRASH COMPACTORS

Trash compactors reduce dry household garbage (glass, cans, bones, plastic, and paper) to less than one-tenth of its original volume and compress it into neat packages. For instance, the weekly dry trash of a family of four, which is about the volume of fourteen kitchen receptacles, can be compressed into a bag weighing about twenty pounds.

Trash compactors are available in a range of sizes — 12, 15, or 18 inches wide, and are installed under the counter. The compactors use between 2300 and 3000 pounds of force to compress trash in less than a minute.

Most trash compactors are activated by the use of a key. The removable key also locks the compactor's motor when the job is completed. In the Frigidaire trash compactor you can interrupt the operating cycle by turning the key to the off position. The General Electric Monogram compactor has a door latch which prevents operation when the door is open. There are also various safety locks on the trash compactors to prevent small children from operating them.

The 18-inch KitchenAid trash compactor has a separate compartment called Litter Bin® that lets you load small items into it while the compactor is operating.

Many trash compactors, such as the KitchenAid and Whirlpool models, have a foot pedal that can be used to open the unit when both hands are full. Typically, trash compactors have an anti-jam mechanism which prevents the unit from operating if it is improperly loaded or if trash is trapped.

In the past odors have been a problem with trash compactors, especially those used by small families where the compactor is not operated frequently. To alleviate this problem, renewable air fresheners or charcoal filters with odor control fans have been added to the compactors.

8
Kitchen Storage

Kitchen cabinets determine the style and the functionality of a kitchen. With the wide variety of cabinet styles on the market today, you can choose almost any decor for your kitchen, regardless of whether the cabinets are traditional wood ones or European styled sleek laminates. There is a design to suit everyone's taste, if you look hard enough.

Our grandmothers' kitchens were not showplaces, but they usually had ample storage space, either in a pantry or on open shelves in the kitchen. The storage space was ample because our grandmothers did not have the array of cooking utensils and small electrical appliances that are available today.

Kitchens that are easy to work in have a clear and logical system of storage. Cabinets have been designed and placed so that they store items close to the area where they will be needed. If this is not the case in your kitchen, some rearranging of cabinet contents will make cooking, baking, and cleanup easier and more pleasurable. One kitchen design expert suggests taking everything out of the kitchen cabinets, placing the items on the floor, and then rearranging them. I think you can do the same thing with pencil and paper, plotting the storage areas and then rearranging them.

CABINETS

Kitchen cabinets can be either custom built, modular (stock cabinets), or built on site. There are about 200 manufacturers of kitchen cabinets pro-

ducing cabinets in a wide range of price and quality. Some manufacturers offer both custom and modular. Custom built cabinets are more expensive than modular ones and also can be more expensive than those built on the job by a local carpenter. Industry experts say that as much as one-third of the cost of a new kitchen or a remodeled one is in cabinets.

Custom cabinets are made to your size specifications for your kitchen. With the great number of kitchen cabinet manufacturers, cabinets are available in almost any wood or laminate, door style, and size you want. The cabinets are crafted and finished in the factory. Many of the wood cabinets are hand rubbed with various finishes.

With a custom manufacturer, your cabinets are not made until you place your specific order. They are produced of the wood or laminate you choose and are specifically made to your width, depth, and height specifications, even if these are out of the ordinary. Custom made cabinets can also provide storage space for uniquely shaped items as well as fitting into problem areas in your kitchen.

Another advantage to custom made cabinets is the ability of a large manufacturer to control the consistency and quality of materials used. For instance, Wood-Mode, as well as Quaker Maid and other high quality cabinet manufacturers, controls the entire manufacturing process from the selection and kiln-drying of premium furniture woods to the final hand rubbed finishing.

Most of the large manufacturers of kitchen

cabinets have authorized dealers throughout the country who are trained by the factory to assist you in kitchen planning and layout. These dealers usually have sample cabinets on display so that you can closely inspect the workmanship and finish of the cabinets.

There are also semi-custom cabinets available which are not as expensive as custom cabinets, but provide some of the same features. For example, Quaker Maid's Coronado line of cabinets, which includes wood and laminate doors, use stock size cabinet boxes with custom-made facades and doors. Although the cabinet boxes do not have the dove-tailed construction of custom cabinets, they are very substantial. Many of the custom features are incorporated in Quaker Maid's semi-custom cabinets. These include glass fronted wall cabinets; wine rack; planning desk; corner lazy Susan base cabinet; ventilation hood; microwave oven shelf; open corner cabinets; and laminated doors combined with sculptured oak door and drawer pulls.

Modular or stock cabinets are produced in a factory to "standard" specifications and then warehoused until ordered. While these cabinets may be better than some built on the job, they have several disadvantages. For example, modular or stock cabinets are manufactured to "standard" sizes. Thus it becomes necessary to plan your kitchen to fit the cabinets instead of the other way around. Also, there are frequently smaller choices in finishes, designs, hardware, and special storage cabinets in stock cabinets.

Modular cabinets are manufactured in 3-inch increments, usually starting with a very narrow 9-inch cabinet for trays. Double door cabinets are as wide as 48 inches. All modular base cabinets are 24 inches deep and wall cabinets are 12 inches deep.

Cabinets built on the job are made to fit the available space by a local carpenter. They are assembled and finished on the job site. Their quality and versatility of storage space depends on the craftsman.

TYPES OF CABINETS

There are three types of cabinets — base, wall, and special purpose. Base cabinets perform dual functions by combining storage space with countertop work surfaces. Standard equipment of base cabinets is one drawer and one shelf with a door. However, they can be configured to two, three, or four drawers, as well as various pull-out shelves. In the case of corner cabinets, a revolving lazy Susan can be installed.

The standard height of base cabinets is 36 to 37 inches depending on the thickness of the countertop. This is based on 30½ inches of cabinet, plus 4½ inches for the toe or kick plate and 1 inch for the countertop. If you are short, as I am, you can cut the height of the toe space to lower the cabinets a little. You can also increase the height of the toe space to raise the cabinets. However, in the area where the dishwasher is to be installed, there is little room to lower the cabinets since dishwashers are 33 $^{11}/_{16}$ inches in height and they are installed under the countertop.

A tile countertop set in mortar on top of a plywood base will make the cabinets higher than a laminate on top of the same plywood base. The difference in height is about ¾ to 1 inch, depending on the thickness of tile and the amount of mortar used to set it. It is not recommended to set tile in mastic for a kitchen counter because repeated use of water on the countertops can loosen the tile.

Wall cabinets, as the name implies, are mounted on the wall. They can also be hung from the ceiling for peninsula installations. Wall cabinets range from 12 to 15 inches deep and are 12 to 33 inches high. The 12-inch high wall cabinets are usually placed over a refrigerator. Custom wall cabinets can be higher than 33 inches to eliminate the open space between the top of the wall cabinets and the ceiling.

I have a 9 foot 4 inch ceiling in the kitchen and have opted to have the cabinets built to the ceiling because I found in a previous kitchen that anything stored on top of wall cabinets was not only un-

Quaker Maid's Coronado semi-custom cabinets in Brookshire styling featuring glass-fronted wall cabinets, wine rack, and planning desk. Photo courtesy of Quaker Maid.

sightly but also a dust catcher. On the other hand, many people prefer the openness the space creates and use it to display collections of plates, baskets, jugs, and other decorative items.

Many kitchens have peninsulas that divide the kitchen from the eating area. Ceiling mounted cabinets above the peninsula often have doors on both sides of the cabinets so that dishes can be put into one side and taken from the other side to set the table. Although these cabinets above the peninsula provide extra storage space, I have found that they make the entire area look smaller and give the kitchen as well as the dining area a closed-in feeling. This arrangement also prevents conversation between the cook and the people in the dining area.

Special purpose cabinets are those that are designed with cutouts for appliances. Special base cabinets provide housing for drop-in-ranges, dishwashers, trash compactors, and under-the counter refrigerators, freezers, or icemakers. Base cabinets are also available with cutouts for sinks and cooktops. These cutout base cabinets usually do not contain a shelf, but may have a flip-out utility drawer. A tall one unit cabinet is designed with cutouts for one or two wall ovens, and a tall, wide wall cabinet can also be designed to house a built-in 24-inch deep refrigerator. There are special wall cabinets for microwave ovens.

European Designed Cabinets

European designs have influenced cabinetry as well as kitchen appliances. This type of design is available from American manufacturers and from European manufacturers, many of whom have plants in the United States.

European cabinets do not have a face frame or border that separates the doors and drawers as is commonly found in many American cabinets. A face frame gives cabinets an early American or traditional look but blocks 15 to 20% of the cabinet's interior. The doors of the cabinets meet flush and this creates a sleeker, more modern-looking cabinet.

European cabinets have a wide variety of internal fittings that make space more efficient. For example, there is a pull-out basket in the cabinet under the sink that is designed for soap products and sponges. The pivotable shelf that brings a heavy mixer or food processor from inside the cabinet to counter height was a European innovation.

In European cabinet design the kick space is independent of the cabinets. This allows the height of the cabinets to vary according to the height of the cook.

CABINET MATERIALS

Today's kitchen cabinets are available in three basic surface materials — wood, laminates, and steel. Of the three, wood cabinets are the most popular with laminates not far behind. The price of wood cabinets greatly depends on the kind of wood used, with birch, pine, and oak being less costly than cherry or mahogany.

If you are considering wood cabinets make sure that the finish is durable for good looking cabinets through the years. Inexpensive cabinets are often finished by printing a wood-grained pattern on plain particleboard or plywood.

Since birch and oak are the hardest woods and the most durable they are the most popular for kitchen cabinets. The appearance of these cabinets can be greatly varied not only with the door styles, but also the stain used. For instance, the stains used on Quaker Maid's birch cabinets range from a Frosty White and Sandrift Beige to Natural. Oak, which shows more of the wood grain, is given stains that range from a very light Sandrift White, to Natural to warm Cinnamon and Nutmeg. There are eight tones in Quaker Maid's cherry stains from a light brown Fawn to a deep toned Claret.

For a lighter contemporary look, many cabinet manufacturers offer white, gray, or beige pigmented stains. Quaker Maid has a Frosty White finish for their birch cabinets which gives them an enameled appearance.

Wood veneers can also be used for cabinets that have no raised panel doors. This contemporary look can be further enhanced with light stains on the wood. Alno, the German cabinet manufacturer with a plant in Delaware, has combined ash veneers with a charcoal stain to bring out the grain of the wood. The cabinets have a Mother of Pearl finish for durability.

Each kitchen cabinet manufacturer offers a variety of woods from which to choose. Wood-Mode, for instance, offers four woods — cherry, maple, oak, and pine. The pine is crafted into a country look, which is enhanced by a distressed finish and occasional knots in the wood, but the cabinets use 20th century hardware for efficiency. For an additional decorative accent, Wood-Mode offers hand stenciling designs which can be applied to their painted cabinets.

If purchasing stock or less expensive cabinets, be sure to see if the parts of the cabinets that show are made of the same wood as the doors. For example, if the doors are cherry and the face frame is maple, over the years the two will age differently, even if they look alike at the beginning.

The finishing process on more expensive cabinets can involve as many as twelve or more steps with some hand rubbing after each. Most manufacturers who produce cabinets in the medium to higher price range use a catalyzed conversion varnish that is applied over whatever stain is chosen. This type of finish is literally baked on for durability. It is resistant to moisture and skin oils and is impervious to common household chemicals such as ammonia, window cleaner, and vinegar.

Lacquer finishes on wood cabinets are easier to apply and cheaper, but tend to be less durable since they chip off or nick. However, Alno has an extremely durable and chip resistant high gloss lacquer finish on their painted cabinets. Alno's lacquered cabinets of high density fiberboard come in matte or high gloss finishes. Lacquered cabinets also provide the opportunity for very subtle fashion colors as in Alno's Alnotess lacquered Jasmine cabinets. The color is white with just a hint of peach, giving the kitchen a very soft look.

Lacquer finishes do not have to be shiny as evidenced in Alno's Alnobel cabinets which have a gray matte lacquer finish. Hardwood countertops can be combined with the matte finish for a contemporary look.

The most durable of all finishes are laminates. Even if your heart is set on a wood kitchen, but you have small children and want durability, do not despair. There are many wood grained laminates available which are hard to distinguish from the real thing. Laminates create a modern atmosphere and give you a wide range of color choices, from pure white to vibrant red.

Laminates are often combined on door panels with either wood trim or sculptured wooden bars at the top or bottom of drawers and doors for easy opening. Wood trim also softens the sleek look of laminated cabinets and gives them a very elegant look. Laminates are available in various textures for visual interest, as well as matte or high gloss finishes.

Construction of Cabinets

Since kitchen cabinets are a major investment, they must stand up under heavy use day after day. In the average kitchen there are many drawers and cabinets that are used more than once a day. I use the eating utensil drawer every time I set the table for a meal and the cooking utensil drawer is used every time I cook. Plates from a cabinet are used both in cooking and serving.

Solid wood is not ideally suited for large flat surfaces such as cabinet sides, bottoms, and shelves where stability is needed. Since there is a tendency for wood to expand and contract with humidity, wide expanses of solid wood tend to warp and split. According to Wood-Mode, the material best suited for this purpose is tightly compressed wood, called flakeboard. The flakeboard serves as a perfect base for wood veneers on large

Alno's Alnofresh kitchen cabinets of ash veneer in charcoal with a mother-of-pearl finish. Photo courtesy of Alno Kitchen Cabinets, Inc.

Alno's Alnotess lacquered kitchen cabinets in Jasmine, a white with a touch of peach. The countertops are a laminate in granite design. Photo courtesy of Alno Kitchen Cabinets, Inc.

An early American kitchen with fireplace for cooking with cast iron pots and pans.

Kitchen of the late 1920s to early 1930s, with early refrigerator and cookstove on legs. Ford Museum, Dearborn, MI.

Dream kitchen of the 1940s with continuous countertops and a streamlined look. Ford Museum, Dearborn, MI.

Antique table is used as a work surface in this country kitchen with Monogram appliances. Courtesy of General Electric.

Brielle white laminate kitchen in European styling with red accents. Courtesy of Quaker Maid.

Formica® laminates in shades of gray with rose accent featured on the cabinets, countertops, and appliances. Courtesy of Formica® Corp.

Pearl gray Birdseye laminate combines with black for a functional, chic, and sophisticated city apartment kitchen. Courtesy of Quaker Maid.

Double sink installed in the island with counter space around it. Courtesy of Quaker Maid.

Cooktop is lowered in island, providing a separate dining area. Courtesy of Kraft Maid.

Commercial 60-inch gas range for home use.
Courtesy of Garland.

AGA cookstove. Courtesy of AGA.

◄ Southwestern design kitchen with ceran
glass-ceramic cooktop by Schott America.
Courtesy of Schott America.

Chantal enamel-on-steel cookware.
Courtesy of Chantal by Lentrade, Inc.

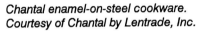

Solid disk cooktop. Two of the disks have
sensors that monitor temperature.
Courtesy of General Electric.

Modular six burner electric cooktop. Courtesy of Jenn-Air.

Trim-Fit® spice drawer insert. Courtesy of Vance Industries.

A cookbook storage area. Photo by Susan Riley.

Hospitality center with under-counter refrigerator and double bar sink. Courtesy of Wood-Mode.

Pull-out hardwood chopping block. Courtesy of Quaker Maid.

Euro-styled built-in refrigerator with wood panels to match cabinets. Courtesy of Sub-Zero.

Under-the-counter mount stainless steel sinks combined with a solid surface countertop for a contemporary look. Courtesy of Franke, Inc.

Sunline sink created by Luigi Colani. Courtesy of Franke, Inc.

European-style round preparation sink with cutting board and drain basket. Courtesy of Abbaka.

Laminated door fronts combined with wood trim drawer and door pulls: Sierra Traditional kitchen. Courtesy of Kraft Maid.

Island with sink and eating area. Photo by Susan Riley.

Kitchen with Designer Solarian floor. Courtesy of Armstrong World Industries, Inc.

exposed surfaces. Flakeboard is also the base for durable laminates on Wood-Mode's cabinet interiors.

Sheets of pressed wood are also used by other cabinet manufacturers for large expanses and for laminate door bases. This type of wood can be bent for curved surfaces to which laminates are applied.

Curved surfaces in cabinets add warmth and softness to a mass of kitchen cabinets. They also make traffic flow easier and more efficient. Special machinery, heat, and moisture are used to bend solid oak doors and panels under pressure to achieve curved cabinets, such as the Wexford collection by Quaker Maid.

There are several construction features that make cabinets stand up to a great deal of wear and tear. Sturdy cabinet doors that fit snugly against the cabinet will not only stand up to continual use but will also be tight enough to prevent dust from creeping into the cabinets. Top quality drawers are constructed of solid hardwood with dovetail or tongue-and-groove joints in all four corners. If these are not available on the cabinets you are contemplating using, then look for a combination of glue and nails in the drawer construction. The sturdiest cabinets have hardwood frames that are ¾ to 1 inch thick with mortise and tenon joints.

Hardware such as hinges and drawer slides take most of the wear of a cabinet. Merillat invented and pioneered the first self-closing hinges that are now a standard item on most manufactured cabinets. Self-closing hinges eliminate the need for magnetic catches.

Drawer slides range from simple nylon bearing surfaces to three-piece steel slides with ball bearings. On medium to higher priced cabinets the drawer slides extend the drawer's full length with no side to side movement as the drawer is being used.

Cabinet interiors should be smooth and preferably have laminated drawers and shelves for easy cleaning. The laminates can either contrast or complement the cabinets' exteriors. Wood-Mode uses natural wood grain laminates which coordi-

nate with the exterior of the cabinets. Shelf paper does not need to be used on laminate interiors.

Half inch shelving is adequate, but ¾ inch is better. The former should not be used in shelves over 36 inches long. Adjustable shelving is a must in kitchen cabinets. Although you will not be changing shelf positions that often, adjustable shelves are essential when storing awkward items.

There are various pull-out shelf configurations available, which provide easy access to pantry goods and cooking utensils. Swing-out shelves for pantries are also available.

PROBLEM STORAGE AREAS

With the availability of custom kitchen cabinets not an inch of space in the kitchen needs to be wasted. For better storage there are pull-out trays, deep pop-up equipment drawers for small appliances, lazy Susans that swing deep into hidden corners, and customized pantries that provide a great deal of storage space.

One of the areas where storage space has been wasted in the past is in the corners where cabinets meet. This is true of both base and wall cabinets. Lazy Susans or carousels can be installed in both corner and catty-corner cabinets to provide easy access storage space. In the corner cabinet a part of the lazy Susan can be cut out like a pie wedge to accommodate the revolving corner door. Thirty-six inches of wall space in both directions are required for this type of revolving shelves in a corner base cabinet.

Lazy Susans can be installed in both the corner base cabinet and the upper cabinet. Since the width of the wall cabinet is smaller, the door does not revolve, but merely opens to one side. An appliance garage can be installed under the upper cabinet to take advantage of the deep counter space.

Lazy Susans, however, do not have to be confined to corner cabinets. When installed in a wall they provide easy access to condiment bottles and jars, as well as other food staples.

This closeup of a Quaker Maid base corner cabinet shows the pie cutout with cabinet door attached in the back. As the lazy Susan turns, the door will be back in position at the front of the cabinet. Photo courtesy of Quaker Maid.

Above the revolving base cabinet, Quaker Maid has installed revolving shelves in the upper cabinet which is above an appliance garage. Photo courtesy of Quaker Maid.

The concept of the double base swing-out corner cabinet was developed by Quaker Maid. After opening the main cabinet door, the left hand unit swings out with two shelves attached to it. When this has cleared the opening, a second shelf unit can also be swung out, leaving both in view at the same time. The shelves can be used to store pantry goods or cooking utensils.

Another problem storage area is the cabinet over the refrigerator which is often only 12 inches deep. By making the cabinet 24 inches deep, you can have more space to store seldom used items. For the new 24-inch deep refrigerators this enlarged cabinet provides a built-in look.

The space behind the toe kick is completely wasted in most kitchens. Plain'n Fancy Cabinets have solved this problem by using this space for a low drawer. The drawer front is in line with the rest of the base cabinet, but part of the drawer is indented to accommodate the toe space.

Alno, Wood-Hu, and other manufacturers have a step stool that folds and stores in the kickboard

Alno's corner pantry cabinet in the Alnotann natural spruce. Photo courtesy of Alno Kitchen Cabinets, Inc.

A narrow tall pantry with adjustable shelves, pull-out shelves, and sliding wire racks. A spice rack is in the door. Photo courtesy of Quaker Maid.

of base cabinets. The top of the ladder has the kickboard attached to it. A pull-out handle on the kickboard makes it easy to reach the ladder.

PANTRY STORAGE

Many of us dream about having a walk-in pantry. It is a large closet with shelves on the three interior walls for the storage of food staples and extra equipment. The more realistic version of this pantry, however, is a pantry cabinet with either pull-out or swing-out shelves. This can be a single, double, or triple affair, with shelves in the doors and swing-out units in the cabinet. A pantry cabinet can also have pull-out or stationary shelves, even in a corner cabinet.

The pantry cabinet can be the full height of the combined base and wall cabinets with swing-out and adjustable shelves, such as the Chef's Pantry designed by Wood-Mode. For a smaller space there is a compact version of the same pantry which fits into a base cabinet.

A narrow pantry can be versatile with a combination of storage units. Adjustable shelves in a tall pantry cabinet make it easy to accommodate items of differing heights. Roll-out shelves bring items into easy view and sliding wire racks are ideal for bottle storage. Table linens can be neatly stored on closely spaced roll-out shelves in a narrow pantry.

A small space, such as 36 inches, can provide big storage with a double door pantry that has shelves in the doors for storage of canned goods. Swing-out shelves provide easy access to items stored in the back of the cabinet. Pull-out drawers beneath the pantry store linens and a wine rack is located above the pantry.

Foodstuffs are easily available in a pantry with pull-out drawers. These pull-out drawers give you an instant overview of your canned goods and staples. I have found that storing canned goods on their sides on low pull-out shelves gives me a better look at them.

Racks of various sizes are ideal for pantry storage. A pull-out rack with adjustable baskets fits into a tall pantry. Packaged and canned foods fit conveniently into an adjustable rack on a cabinet door.

A bread box with a cover can help keep bakery goods and bread fresh. This unit is installed in a deep drawer and should be in a bank of cabinets that is away from a heat source. Some cabinet manufacturers, such as Merillat, have tin-lined bread boxes. Crackers and cereal can also be stored in a bread box. Most bread drawers have either a tin or acrylic cover over the bread box.

Spices are another item that should be stored away from heat so that they will not lose their potency. They may either be placed in a specially designed drawer or on racks on the inside of a cabinet door. The specially designed spice drawer with an angled shelf insert keeps spices tilted so that their labels are easy to see and read.

Spice racks can be placed on the inside of cabinet doors that house pantry items or frequently used condiments. Wood-Mode has a spice rack that mounts on the back of a cabinet door. Spices can also be stored on a lazy Susan in a wall cabinet. The

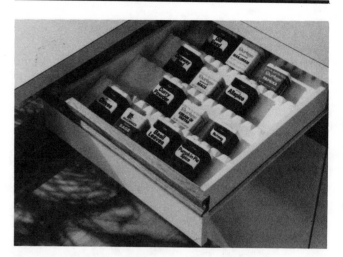

Drawer with specially designed rack for spices. Cabinet by Quaker Maid. Photo courtesy of Quaker Maid.

spices should be located close to the food preparation area. As stated earlier, some cooks also like to keep a duplicate set of the most frequently used spices in a drawer or on a shelf adjacent to the cooktop.

Vance Industries produces spice dividers of various widths for kitchen drawers. They are also available with large and small compartments.

Custom vegetable drawers of various types are produced by many cabinet manufacturers. Wood-Mode makes a wooden vegetable drawer for a base cabinet with a perforated bottom panel for ventilation. Merillat and Kraft Maid have base cabinets with plastic coated pull-out wire baskets for root vegetable storage. The use of perforated drawers and wire or plastic bins for vegetable storage in base cabinets allows cooler air (it is cooler at the bottom of a room than at the top, since warm air rises) to circulate keeping potatoes and onions from sprouting. Wood-Mode also produces a base cabinet for vegetables, with removable tote trays that are easily carried to the preparation area.

If you have a specific area in your kitchen you use for baking, pull-out plastic or wooden flour bins can be installed in a cabinet under the countertop. One of these bins could be covered with a pull-out wooden cutting board for additional pastry-making space.

APPLIANCE STORAGE

The increased use of small electric kitchen appliances in the last decade has created the need for new storage space. A variety of specialty storage units has been produced by the cabinet makers to house many of these appliances. The most versatile one is an appliance garage which can store a variety of small appliances on the countertop within easy reach but out of sight when not in use.

An appliance garage is an enclosed cabinet installed between the base and wall cabinets, an area usually anywhere from 15 to 18 inches in height. It can be used to store a food processor, mixer, blender, toaster oven, or coffee maker. Appliance garages may be placed on the countertop in a corner or along a straight wall. If installed in the corner, allow 24 inches of wall space from each corner. The straight appliance garages, which are the same depth as the wall cabinets, are available in 18, 24, 30 or 36-inch lengths or can be custom-made to any length.

To be able to use the appliances stored in the garage quickly, electrical connections should be installed in the garage or outside close to it. Many appliances have short cords so that they will not work conveniently if the plugs are a distance away. Either a roll-up tambour or a swing-up or swing-out door hides appliances when they are not in use. If a tambour door is used on the garage, the door is hidden in the top of the cabinet when the garage is open.

Special cabinets are also designed for microwave ovens. They are part of a wall cabinet and designed to put the controls of the oven at eye level. This type of cabinet removes a free-standing microwave from the counter and gives it a built-in look. By using a wall installation for your microwave oven you can utilize the counter space below it for preparation of dishes going into the oven. Kraft Maid makes a standard 18-inch shelf for microwave ovens.

A base cabinet with a mixer lift keeps a bulky, heavy mixer practically at your fingertips for instant use. The shelf on which the mixer is stored lifts out and up to working height. It is also easily retracted into its hideaway position without the need to handle the appliance. In many of the units, such as ones by Kraft Maid, Wood-Mode, and Quaker Maid, there is a roll-out drawer beneath the mixer shelf to store measuring cups, mixer attachments, or a blender.

Pull-out shelves in base cabinets can also be used for small appliance storage, particularly if the appliance tends to be heavy like a large food processor.

Cooks have mixed feelings about leaving small appliances on countertops. Some say that it creates a cluttered look, others insist that they would never use these appliances if they had to get them out of a cabinet. I have tried it both ways and like storing most small appliances in cabinets or drawers since it gives my kitchen a neater look.

PREPARATION STORAGE

Many kitchen cabinet manufacturers provide drawers with partitions to organize cooking utensils and knifes neatly . For example, utility drawers by Wood-Mode and Kraft Maid provide knife inserts with space for a dozen utility knives. These knife inserts will also fit larger drawers with additional space for other cooking utensils. Many other manufacturers have cutlery drawers which can be organized for cooking or eating utensils.

Knives used in food preparation can be stored in various other ways. They should not be allowed to rattle around in drawers since that will dull the blades. For custom-made cabinets and countertops, an area with slots for knives can be designed near the sink, the cooktop, or the preparation area. In my previous kitchen, I had a slot for preparation knives built into the wall near the sink and adjacent to the preparation area.

Magnetic racks or slotted wooden blocks which either sit on the countertop or hang on the wall are most common for knife storage. Another attractive and efficient alternative is to build a knife holder at the end of a counter. It is especially convenient built into a butcher block island. However, this type of knife storage is not recommended to a household with small children.

Vance Industries produces compartmentalized utility trays of various sizes for kitchen drawers. They can be used for utensils or cutlery and can be trimmed to fit most standard cabinet drawers. The trays also come in two layers, one sliding over the other to provide extra storage space.

Cutting boards of various types can be part of the kitchen cabinetry. Pull-out hardwood chopping blocks are stored just below the countertop for easy access. It can also double as an extra work space. Quaker Maid also makes a laminated pull out work surface which adds 30 inches of additional work surface and is capable of supporting 100 pounds.

Wood-Mode has a pull-out counter with a scratch-resistant surface as a standard feature in their bar cabinet. The counter also provides additional work space.

Vance Industries' Surface Savers® of various tempered glass designs can be installed in the kitchen countertop to provide a cutting board. The white or almond surface, which is mounted in a stainless steel frame, is also heat resistant. The surface can be used for chopping, slicing, and dicing without leaving any scratches or cuts.

COOKING AND BAKING UTENSIL STORAGE

Pots, pans, roasters, Dutch ovens, stock pots, casseroles, baking sheets, and cake pans are all bulky items requiring large storage areas. As I keep emphasizing, these storage areas should be near where the item is to be used. Since many of the pots and pans are heavy, they should be stored in a base cabinet where they will be easier to lift up and out.

Pull-out shelves or large drawers seem to provide the most efficient storage space for pots and pans. They can either be vinyl coated wire or solid shelves. Alno makes two special kitchen cabinets for cooking and baking utensils. One is a set of four drawers designed to be installed below a cooktop for easy access to pots and pans. The other is also a drawer that is installed below a wall oven. It has an adjustable shelf above the open drawer space that provides storage for a broiler pan. The drawer can be used for large casseroles and other baking equipment.

A pot rack over the cooktop provides easy access to often used cooking utensils. It can also be an attractive focal point in the kitchen and does not have to display only one type of pot or pan. Copper, iron, and stainless steel as well as colorful enameled pots can be mixed for an attractive display.

Many cabinet manufacturers produce special racks, which either fit into cabinet drawers or can be pulled out of a wall cabinet, to hold pot lids. Wood-Mode has drawer dividers that are interchangeable with drawers of the same size.

Large pots and pans used for steaming should be stored near the sink to make it easy to fill them for cooking.

Baking pans, cookie sheets, and other flat items, such as trays, are best stored in an upright position. Dividers in either base or wall cabinets can provide slotted storage space for these items. The wall cabinet above the oven is deeper than other wall cabinets and can also be used to store these flat items. Kraft Maid produces wire tray dividers which can be inserted into these types of cabinet.

Trays can also be stored in a base cabinet with dividers. The use of vertical dividers, slanted in the front, in a base cabinet makes it easier to find your favorite tray.

Corner cabinet with swing-out shelves provides storage for cooking utensils in Alno's pearlized white Alnofresh cabinets. Photo courtesy of Alno Kitchen Cabinets, Inc.

Four drawers below the cooktop store pots and pans. Cabinet by Alno. Photo by Alno Kitchen Cabinets, Inc.

CLEANUP STORAGE

Cleanup supplies such as dishwasher powder, soap, scouring pads, and waste disposal should be close to the sink. Depending on whether you have a waste disposer and a trash compactor there should be a facility to handle both soft and solid garbage.

Many cabinet manufacturers make a tilt-out utility tray in the base cabinet just below the sink for cleaning utensils, sponges, and soap. This fold-down drawer can have one or two trays depending on the width of the sink.

Pull-out vinyl-coated wire racks that fit into the sink cabinet are available to store a variety of cleaning supplies. However, this type of storage is only feasible under a sink that does not have a waste disposer.

Dish towels can be kept within easy reach on an under the counter pull-out rack.

Most people use the cabinet under the sink for both the cleaning supplies and some sort of garbage disposal. Many kitchen cabinet manufacturers have produced special cabinets or racks for the cleanup area. For example, Alno has a carousel trash container that fits under the sink and has two compartments for various types of trash or garbage. When the cabinet door is opened, the trash container swings forward for easy access. Alno also makes double waste bins that swing out when the cabinet door under the sink is opened.

There are many special pull-out cabinets designed specifically as a waste basket. In the Quaker Maid waste basket cabinet, the plastic trash container lifts out for easy removal. Similar cabinets are also available from St. Charles and Wood-Mode.

Tilt-out cleanup tray. Cabinet by Quaker Maid. Photo courtesy of Quaker Maid.

Carousel Trash Container segments the trash. It swings out when the cabinet door is opened. Cabinet by Alno. Photo courtesy of Alno Kitchen Cabinets, Inc.

Stem glass holder above a small bar sink in the hospitality area of the kitchen. Cabinet by Kraft Maid. Photo courtesy of Kraft Maid.

WINE STORAGE

Wine bottles should be stored on their sides to keep the cork wet, which helps keep the wine from spoiling. Although ideally wine should be stored in a controlled temperature between 52 and 58 degrees F., many cooks like to display their wine selection. Whenever the wine rack is placed in the kitchen, it should be in the coolest part of the room.

A cabinet especially designed for wine storage with crisscross slots for bottles of wine can be installed under the countertop or as a wall unit. A wine rack also is an attractive display at the end of the center island or peninsula in the kitchen near the hospitality center.

Stem glasses can be attractively displayed in a specially designed glass holder for easy access. This glass holder attaches to the bottom of an upper cabinet and can be installed on a wall-mounted cabinet or a cabinet over a peninsula.

SOME SPECIALLY DESIGNED STORAGE UNITS

There are a number of unique storage units to fit specific needs. For example, if you have a desk in the kitchen there is a file drawer available for it.

Custom range hoods can be perfectly matched to the woods and finishes of kitchen cabinets. These are usually wall cabinets which are installed over a cooktop along a wall and cannot be used over an island or peninsula. A fan and a light are concealed in the hood. However, a specially designed hood to match the cabinets is also available for placement over an island or peninsula.

If you like to display collectibles, antiques, or china pieces in your kitchen, attractive plate rails for the tops of wall cabinets are available from such manufacturers as Quaker Maid.

Pull out tables, such as those manufactured by Wood-Mode, can serve several purposes. These tables open to 54 inches and can provide extra work space, a dining table, or a menu planning area.

Another pull-out storage unit is a hideaway serving cart. This serving cart rolls from room to room and fits snugly under the counter where it appears as part of the cabinetry when not in use.

9
Materials and Lighting for the Kitchen

The materials used for countertops, floors, walls, and cabinets will not only determine the style and decor of your dream kitchen, but also its practicality. The selection of materials can ultimately make the cleanup and maintenance of your kitchen a pleasure or a chore. However, many cooks do not mind using a little more maintenance effort to achieve the overall desired atmosphere.

MATERIALS

Over the years kitchen materials have been improved for easier maintenance. Some materials, which had gone out of style, have come back with "easy care" finishes. Linoleum, popular in the early 1900s, is now being imported from Europe and is again being used for kitchen floors. Wood floors, the only kitchen flooring in colonial days, are in vogue, but with a polyurethane "easy care" finish. Rubber-based tiles used to be popular, but have been surpassed by vinyl ones.

Today there is a wide choice of materials for every surface in the kitchen. However, restrictions and the limiting properties of these materials often dictate their usage. Many of the materials used in a kitchen are multipurpose. They can be used on cabinets as well as countertops, or countertops as well as floors.

Many different materials can be combined in a kitchen for a pleasing overall effect. For example, brick and wallpaper can be used on the walls. Brick makes an attractive surround for the cooktop. Wooden cabinets give a warm feeling and coordi-

nate well with the brick. Vinyl flooring and solid surface countertops add easy care to the kitchen.

There is a basic point to note about some of these materials if they are used for flooring. Quarry tile, brick and clay pavers, marble, and ceramic tile should be set in mortar for a long lasting floor. Consequently a strong subfloor is required.

Ceramic Tile

USES: FLOORS, WALLS, AND COUNTERTOPS

Ceramic tile is almost as old as the beginning of civilization and as new as modern high technology methods of production. It can be used on floors, countertops, and walls in a kitchen. Ceramic tile surfaces are nonflammable, nonabsorbent, easy to clean, resistant to household chemicals, and stand up under daily wear.

Ceramic tile is a mixture of clay and water that is fired at a high temperature. The hardened pieces of tile can be glazed, decorated, or left untreated. The methods used to produce the tile determine its type, looks, and care.

There are two types of tiles, unglazed and glazed. The unglazed tile is one color throughout and can be left in a natural tone from cream to umber, or the clay mixture can be tinted with minerals. These tiles are hard wearing and can be used indoors or outdoors. If used in the kitchen they should have a sealer on them to avoid stains.

Glazed tiles are the most widely used and, as their name implies, they have a finish, either matte or shiny. The finish is produced by double firing the tile with the second firing done after the color or design and glaze is applied. Glazed tiles can also have an uneven or pebbly texture. Today there are tiles that imitate marble, granite, stone, and even leather and fabrics. Glazed ceramic tiles are generally used indoors, on countertops, floors, or walls.

Wall tiles are usually the thinnest, being ¼ to ½ inch thick. Floor tiles are thicker, but can be used on walls and countertops as well as floors. However, there are specific tiles made only for floor use.

It is recommended that any tile used on a surface that will occasionally have water on it be set in mortar (called "mud" in the industry) instead of merely using an epoxy adhesive. Kitchen countertops should be set in mortar. However, floor tile can be set in epoxy if wet mopping is only an occasional occurrence and where there is little traffic.

Decorative patterns on ceramic tiles can be hand painted, put on by a silk-screening method, or applied as decals. The tile is fired again after decorating to adhere the decoration to it. Tiles lend themselves beautifully to small designs. For example, I randomly placed 4-inch off-white tiles painted with fruit designs in the backsplash of my counters.

Many designs use several tiles to make up a larger overall design. This can be particularly effective as the backsplash of a cooktop, sink, or baking area. Multi-tile patterns on the floor are particularly effective. However, use of patterns in countertops should be avoided since they become jarring to the eye over time.

There are many different tile accents. Villeroy & Boch, a German-Luxembourg tile manufacturer, makes a rope-like twisted border and a leaded, glass-like, beaded edging. Many of the Italian manufacturers have "designer" lines of tile from well known couture houses or architects. There are also individual artists in many communities who are ceramists and will paint custom designs on tiles. A friend of mine had a large fruit and vegetable basket custom painted as a backsplash for her food preparation center and a selection of breads and sheaves of wheat as the picture for the backsplash of her baking center.

While ceramic tile works well from a wear standpoint, it can be tiring if you stand on it for long periods at a time. Also, glassware, dishes, and crockery break easily when dropped on ceramic tile. Grimy grout lines can be avoided by using a grout that has latex, silicone, or epoxy as part of its formula. I have also found that certain tile designs can be installed with smaller grout lines, thereby alleviating some of the dirt problems.

Ceramic tile can also be used with other countertop materials in the same kitchen, such as butcher block or granite on the center island.

Quarry Tiles

USE: FLOORS

Quarry tile has been available for centuries. It is unglazed and usually comes in earth tones. The tiles come in a variety of thicknesses and sizes. Handmade quarry tiles have a variation within their sizes as well as their colors.

Since quarry tile is very porous, a sealer is usually applied to minimize stains and add a sheen to the tile when it is used indoors. The sealer helps to minimize moisture and helps prevent greasy spills from penetrating the tile.

If the quarry tile is handmade, particularly in Mexico, it is subject to chipping and cracking. American quarry tiles are machine made and tend to be denser. They are also pre-sealed to avoid stains, and some have a hard glossy surface. Quarry tiles are made in squares and hexagons. These tiles tend to be noisy to foot traffic, particularly high heels, and they are hard on the feet over long periods of standing.

Bricks and Clay Pavers

USE: FLOORS

Brick floors and clay pavers add a certain charm to a country kitchen. Both are hard surfaces

Granite on the center island makes a smooth countertop which can be used as a baking center or for buffet service.
Builder: Robert Coruccini. Photo courtesy of Robert Coruccini.

which require a substantial subfloor and should be set in mortar. Both also have a matte finish which is slip resistant.

Pavers resemble brick, but are thinner and usually come in 4 by 8-inch rectangles. Pavers are available in many neutral colors, including grays and terra cotta, and have a sealer which resists stains.

Marble

USES: FLOORS AND COUNTERTOPS

Marble can be used on floors and countertops in the kitchen. It is cool and luxurious and comes in colors ranging from neutral gray, black, and white, to pastel rose, yellow, and blue. The latter two are very difficult to find. The natural veining of marble adds interest to the floor. In the past, marble was always sold in heavy slabs, but for many years it has been available in one foot square tiles. The cost of these marble tiles is comparable to very high quality ceramic tiles.

Most types of marble used in homes are either polished or satin finished. Marble tiles require a well-prepared subsurface and meticulous installation. It is recommended that a professional do the job. Laying marble in an older house may require additional structural support.

Marble requires the same care as fine wood furniture. Spills will stain it and heavy traffic may mar its polished finish. Regular cleaning, polishing, and sealing is necessary to keep the good-looking appearance of a marble floor. A marble floor is slippery when wet and it is also hard and cold, but very beautiful.

Although slightly porous, marble can be used for kitchen countertops. Oil-based substances and harsh spirits will stain it. However, some staining can be alleviated with proper sealing of the surface. The cool surface and smoothness of marble make it ideal for a baking center. Pastry can easily be rolled out on it and the surface is simple to clean.

An elegant kitchen countertop can be ob-tained using marble and under-countertop mounted sinks. Marble can be cut and worked into a rounded edge or a rectangle with rounded corners. For countertop installations marble tiles can be used, but the thicker marble slabs are preferable.

Granite

USE: COUNTERTOPS

Granite is the most durable of all countertops. It looks dramatic and luxurious. Unfortunately, granite ranks among the most expensive of countertop surfaces available.

Since granite comes in large slabs it can be installed without seams or with almost invisible seams, eliminating the grout-cleaning problem. Granite is easy to clean with any household cleaning material. It is particularly heat and scratch resistant.

As with any stone, moisture penetrates granite, but it evaporates without leaving a mark, thus making granite virtually stain resistant. Some types of granite, however, absorb fat, so with that type of granite, it is a good idea to wipe up any fat spots shortly after they occur. To avoid stains, granite tops are treated with an inorganic oil, such as sewing machine oil. This treatment should be repeated periodically.

Granite, like marble, makes an excellent work surface, particularly for baking and candy making. However, it should not be used as a cutting surface because it will dull knives.

Granite countertops, like marble, lend themselves to under-counter sink installations.

Solid Synthetic Surfaces

USE: COUNTERTOPS

In today's dream kitchen it is easy to have a luxurious look with little maintenance. The handsome new solid synthetic surfaces such as Corian®, Surell™ made by the Formica Corporation, and Avonite® provide easy care as well as sleek looking countertops.

These materials are manmade and are a patented blend of natural minerals and acrylics. The solid surfaces combine the elegance of marble and the permanence of stone, yet they have the feature of repairability. Like stone, the texture and pattern of these surfaces go all the way through the material. Since it is a solid material it can be cut and shaped like a fine piece of hardwood.

If there is damage to a countertop it can be repaired. For example Avonite® has a patch kit which fills the damage. The area can then be buffed and polished so that the repair is not noticeable.

Corian®, Surell™, and Avonite® make attractive alternatives to real stone. All three have numerous granite-like patterns as well as a wide range of colors. Solid synthetic surfaces are available in large slabs and are ideal for kitchen islands. These surfaces can also be formed into a "seamless" counter which looks like a single slab of stone. Solid surfaces are available in matte, semi-matte, or high gloss finishes. The solid surfaces cost much less than real stone.

Avonite® is available in straight edge or grid patterns that simulate tile surfaces. To achieve the effect of tile, the precise geometric tile pattern is first cut into the surface and then the grooves are filled with liquid Avonite®. This type of Avonite® countertop provides the look of tile without the disadvantages, such as grout falling out or staining.

Solid surfaces can be inlaid with contrasting colors both on the surface of the countertop and on the edge. For example, an Avonite countertop of granite design can be accented with a dark contrasting inlaid strip. Another Avonite® decorative inlay is a stepped sandwich effect on the counter edge that picks up the accent color in the kitchen.

There are also numerous decorating possibilities with a solid surface. It can be used for countertops in contemporary, traditional, or country kitchens.

There are both advantages and disadvantages to the use of solid synthetics. They are tough, non-porous, non-interactive with household chemicals, and easy to clean. Most stains can be wiped away with a cleanser or scouring pad. These solid surfaces have a higher than average heat resistance. However, hot pots and pans should not be placed directly on the countertop. Although scratches can be removed with a fine scouring pad or fine sandpaper, cutting directly on the countertop is not recommended.

Woods

USES: FLOORS, CABINETS, WALLS, AND BUTCHER BLOCK COUNTERTOPS

Wood can also be used for kitchen floors, cabinets, and as paneling for walls. The use of wood in a kitchen lends a cozy, homey atmosphere to the room.

FLOORS

In early colonial days pine was the prevalent wood used for kitchen flooring. Today oak is used because it is easier to maintain since it is less porous and does not splinter. However, for an authentic country look, soft woods such as pine are still available. These woods come in wide planks and can either be stained or painted with a special floor paint. Over time, the paint will wear away and the floor has to be repainted. A soft wood floor, which is porous, needs a sealer to make it stain resistant. This type of floor needs constant attention to keep it in pristine condition.

Oak floors are much easier to maintain in a kitchen. The flooring is available either in strips or various shapes and sizes of blocks for parquet flooring. The strips are available in standard 2¼-inch widths or in random widths of 3, 5, and 7 inches. Oak flooring is primarily sold in bundles and is available sealed against moisture, stains, and grease. If that is not the case, the floor should be treated with a polyurethane sealer, which may have to be repeated periodically.

To reduce the cost of an oak floor, there are hardwood flooring strips available that are veneers on a plywood base. This type of flooring comes in both the strips and parquet pieces. It is being recommended for houses that have moisture problems since this type of wood flooring will not warp or shrink.

Today's oak floors with special finishes are easy to maintain with vacuuming and occasional damp mopping. A wood floor gives a warm look and is comfortable for long periods of standing.

CABINETS

The majority of cabinet boxes are constructed of wood, as are many of the doors. Doors may be solid wood, with or without raised panels, or pressed wood with a plastic laminated surface. (For a discussion of wood cabinet finishes, see Chapter 8.) Wood cabinets are easy to maintain and, depending on the finish, can either be wiped with a damp cloth, or periodically treated with a cleaning oil. The painted finishes of today's cabinets are very durable and most stains can be wiped off with a damp cloth.

Wood paneling for kitchen walls is available in pre-finished sheets or in planks. Most of the panels consist of veneer on top of plywood or fiberboard. They are textured to resemble planks of wood.

Just as wood cabinets are easy to maintain, so is wood paneling. However, since wood is porous, paneling is not recommended behind the cooktop or the sink where it will absorb cooking moisture and grease.

BUTCHER BLOCK COUNTERTOPS

Butcher block, made of maple or oak, is coming back into style for countertops, especially in country kitchens. It can either be the entire countertop or only a part. Thick solid pieces of wood are usually used for countertops, although extra thick veneer adhered to plywood can be used. The wood must be sealed before using.

Butcher block will stain, is not heat resistant, and will show knife marks. Some people love this latter attribute since it shows wear. Constant use and cleaning breaks down most seals, so that the butcher block must be resealed periodically. It is important to keep the butcher block or hardwood countertop clean because food particles can introduce bacteria into the knife cuts and other nicks in the wood.

Plastic Laminates

USE: COUNTERTOPS AND CABINET FACINGS

Plastic laminates come in a great variety of colors and simulated textures. Photographic techniques have enabled such textures as wood grains, marble, granite, and textile weaves to be reproduced on plastic laminates. In addition to the vast range of colors available in plastic laminates, there are also many geometric patterns. The laminates come in either gloss or matte finishes.

Formica is the name of one of the largest manufacturers of high-pressure laminates and has become almost synonymous with all plastic laminates. The Formica Corporation produces a number of high-pressure laminates such as Formica®,

Wilsonart's laminate Ebony Star simulates granite. Photo of McCombs residence, Temple, TX. Photo courtesy of Ralph Wilson Plastics Co.

Colorcore®, Design Concepts®, and Lacque Metallique®. The Formica® brand of laminates encompasses a wide range of solid colors, patterns, and finishes. Colorcore® is a surfacing material that has uniform solid color throughout the piece. This eliminates dark seams at the edges. The Design Concepts® has a solid color lacquer finish with patterns in a contrasting finish, either matte or gloss. Lacque Metallique® are specially treated one-of-a-kind sheets that are embedded with metallic flakes for reflective effects.

A tambour surface is also produced by Formica and consists of flexible, grooved sheets of laminates. The grooves can be of a contrasting color. This tambour surface can add an interesting texture and pattern to a contemporary kitchen. Since the tambour surface is flexible it can be used on a curved installation.

Plastic laminates can be used on cabinets and countertops. The most popular laminates for cabinets are the wood grains and solid colors. Wilsonart produces laminates that simulate wood grain and can be applied onto raised door panels. Two colors of laminates can be combined for a pleasing visual effect, such as a darker tone for base cabinets and a lighter one for wall cabinets. The cabinet face can be a different color than the door fronts.

Laminates can also be used on a roll-up tambour door to coordinate with the other cabinets in the kitchen. For an accent, a strip may be repeated on the edge of the countertop.

The most widely used kitchen area for laminates is countertops. This is due not only to the wide selection of colors and patterns available, but also the favorable price of laminates. With advanced technology, laminates have become more sophisticated looking. Countertop edges have beveled moldings of like or contrasting color and texture. Laminated countertops can also be set with wood moldings as well as conventional straight edges. Some of these edges can simply be snapped on instead of glued.

Laminates are fairly easy to install using a special adhesive that binds the sheet of laminate to a plywood or pressed wood base. They can be contoured in a special press to curve in the front or up the wall.

Plastic laminated surfaces are easy to clean, and withstand a certain amount of knocks and scratches. However, do not use them as a chopping block and do not place hot dishes on them as they scorch easily.

Stainless Steel

USE: COUNTERTOPS

Stainless steel countertops are preferred by professional cooks because they are hard-wearing, easy to clean, and withstand extremes of heat. They do scratch with use, but many people say that is part of the charm of this surface. Working on stainless steel can be noisy.

Vinyl

USE: FLOORS

Vinyl flooring in a kitchen has come a long, long way since our grandmothers and great-grandmothers first used linoleum – a sheeting material which later spawned vinyl flooring. No longer do vinyl floors damage easily and need a weekly waxing, as did linoleum.

Today vinyl floors are durable, easy to care for, and affordable. Spills wipe up easily from vinyl floors and they are stain resistant but not stain proof. Vinyl floors are comfortable because they are resilient and warm beneath your feet. They are also skid resistant. There is a wide choice of patterns available, from look-alike marble and wood to contemporary motifs and textures.

The disadvantages to vinyl floors are that they can fade or discolor in direct sunlight, and they can be dented or scratched by furniture or appliance movements, and sometimes even by spike heels.

Vinyl comes in two forms, sheets and tiles. The sheet flooring comes in 6- or 12-foot widths and the tiles are usually 12 inches square. With the sheet flooring you can achieve more continuity and a more elegant look. Tiles give you multiple seams and are more difficult to maintain.

Sheet vinyl flooring is manufactured by two types of processes: inlay and rotogravure. In an inlay flooring, the pattern extends through the thickness of the material down to the backing. Vinyl granules are usually applied to the backing by way of a series of templates and then fused together. The higher quality vinyls are then given a protective coating, making the inlaid floors more durable.

In a rotogravure flooring the pattern is printed with vinyl inks onto a mineral-coated felt backing. Then a wear layer is added for protection. Thicker vinyls are not necessarily better made, but the way they are made is what counts. Armstrong, for instance, makes three grades of vinyl flooring and grades them Best, Better, and Good. Designer Solarian is an example of their best grade.

Vinyl tiles can either be solid vinyl or a vinyl composition, which is a mixture of vinyl, clay, and mineral fibers. The latter is the most common type for household use. The tiles are either embossed or printed and some have a protective wear coating.

The protective coating repels dirt and spills and protects the pattern. Most of the wear layer coatings are either polyurethane or vinyl, and both claim to be a no-wax finish. However, both finishes wear off over the years, although the polyurethane coating will last longer.

For a custom, one-of-a-kind flooring you might want to consider vinyl tiles. They can be arranged in any pattern you desire and come in a vast array of colors. With the current great fashion emphasis on black and white, a black and white tile floor is very attractive. Even a rug effect of three or four different colors of tiles can be centered in the kitchen with solid color tiles going around it.

In recent years, vinyl flooring has emulated the natural looks of brick, wood, stone, and ceramic tile. However, there is a trend toward less representational patterns with the European sleek decor.

Carpet

USE: FLOORS

Although carpet is very comfortable under the feet and easy to stand on, I feel that it does not have a place in the kitchen, where food spills frequently hit the floor. An area rug, however, might be used in the dining area of the kitchen to create a more cozy atmosphere.

If you do opt to use carpeting on the kitchen floor, choose one of the short fiber indoor-outdoor types which will not readily attract dirt and can be cleaned. Synthetic fibers are best for this type of carpeting. With carpeted flooring all spills must be wiped up immediately to avoid permanent stains.

Paint and Wallpaper

USES: WALLS AND CEILINGS

Painted walls and ceilings can create a colorful backdrop to your kitchen cabinets, countertops, and floor. Walls and ceilings can be painted with brush or roller. Paint can be applied with rags to simulate an antique look.

Paint is the most inexpensive covering for kitchen walls and ceilings. It is easily applied and is completely washable. Although enamel paint is best for washability and to withstand the normal moisture in the kitchen, latex is preferred. It does not yellow or fade as easily, does not have the glare of enamel, and is easier to apply. Any painted woodwork in the kitchen, however, should be painted with semi-gloss enamel.

Wallpaper comes in many patterns and textures. Vinyl coated wallpaper is easy to maintain and can be washed periodically. It can be applied to walls and ceilings. One of the most attractive kitchens I ever had was one that had a wallpapered ceiling. The design consisted of casual bunches of flowers on an off-white background. The design was so cheerful that it made the kitchen a delightful place to work.

An old-fashioned three-globe light fixture illuminates the center island. Cabinets by Wood-Mode. Photo courtesy of Wood-Mode.

LIGHTING

Just as materials are important in the kitchen, so is proper lighting — whether it is natural or artificial. Attractive kitchen light fixtures can help create a comfortable atmosphere in the kitchen for working as well as dining.

During the day, the best light is natural light. Large windows, skylights, and greenhouse windows provide light that can enhance a kitchen. Bay windows, especially in the breakfast area, will not only provide natural light but can break up any box-like atmosphere that may exist in a kitchen. A greenhouse window can provide not only light but also extra space to display greenery or a collection of pewter, baskets, and other favorite items. Artificial light is often used to supplement daylight, particularly to illuminate dark corners and to light the kitchen during dull days.

Light, whether natural or artificial, is affected by the colors, textures, and various finishes in the kitchen. Pale colors reflect light and dark colors absorb it. Matte surfaces absorb light and glossy surfaces reflect it. The most pleasant lighting in a kitchen is the type where the light sources are not apparent, but create balanced lighting.

Kitchens need some pleasingly bright overall lighting as well as task lighting. However, it is best to avoid using a single central light because it will throw shadows on the counters. Background lighting should not be as important as lighting for the work surfaces. Single recessed ceiling lights, which pivot to throw light where needed, can be used to illuminate specific work areas. Multi-pronged lights can also be used to illuminate a large area, such as the work surface on a center island.

Although lighting options are many, there are only two sources of electric light — fluorescent and incandescent. Fluorescent lights are popular because they use less energy and the bulbs last longer. However, fluorescent lights can make food look unappetizing unless warm-white or halogen bulbs, which closely resemble daylight, are used.

A good rule of thumb for lighting above countertops and work areas is to provide 120 watts of incandescent or 20 watts of fluorescent lighting for each 3 feet of work space. Sinks and cooktops or ranges also need good lighting. Since sinks usually do not have overhead cabinets, recessed ceiling mounted lights can provide good task lighting.

I have a recessed ceiling light over the sink and three over the center island work area. For more diffused and softer lighting we have two Tiffany lamps, one on each end of the island. All of our cabinet counters are illuminated by fluorescent strip lighting under the wall cabinets, each with its own switch.

Track lighting can be used for accent as well as task lighting over an island. By manipulating the individual lights on the track you can eliminate shadows at work areas and create a balanced light which is flattering to food. If you have a very large island, consider using a double track of lights to avoid shadows.

Eating areas require two types of lighting, one for the table top and one for background. For optimum lighting, choose a fixture that incorporates more than one type of illumination. For example, a light fixture with a central light source and several small bulbs around it can provide two types of lighting — general lighting for the diners and spot lighting for the table.

For dining tables, the most popular type of lighting is a hanging fixture. It should hang 30 to 36 inches above the tabletop so that people can easily see each other across the table. The lamp should be centered over the table and be no larger than 12 inches less than the width of the table. Be sure to include a dimmer switch for those cozier occasions.

In choosing light fixtures for the kitchen, try to visualize the amount of artificial light needed on a bright day versus a very dull, rainy afternoon.

10
Kitchen Styles

In the last ten years, technological advances, improvements in the designs of large and small appliances, and the use of softer, more pleasing colors have made kitchens warmer, cozier, and more luxurious. Cabinet and major appliance manufacturers have created designs and efficient functionality to meet the demands of the modern consumer.

The style and decor of your dream kitchen is a matter of personal taste, although it may be governed by the structure of the room and the decor and architectural period of your house. Also consider the surroundings on the outside, since they will be viewed from the kitchen. The patio is an adjunct to the kitchen when entertaining or serving informal family meals.

Kitchens, like clothing, have design trends, but thankfully they do not drastically change as often as clothing. In choosing the style of your kitchen keep in mind that it can be changed, but not as easily as an item of clothing.

EUROPEAN STYLING

One of the most recent design concepts for kitchens is the European look. American companies have been increasingly copying the European features, which include sleek styling, concealed adjustable hinges on cabinets, wire racks, and other space-saving storage systems. The European look in plumbing fixtures and appliances is compact. European styling is based on function — the best and simplest design for the product for its intended task.

European design is not really that new. In the 1940s and '50s motion studies of kitchens were conducted by several major American universities, including Cornell, which recommended the same features that are now present in European style cabinets and appliances. "European styling," in many instances, has become a catch-all phrase for sleek looking, contemporary kitchens.

CONTEMPORARY KITCHENS

As a result of this European styling trend the contemporary style of kitchen has evolved into one which features either monotone soft colors or a prime color with a stark, bright accent. Black and white is a combination frequently used in this type of kitchen. In keeping with the strictly functional theme of these kitchens, few decorative touches are used. Some functional kitchens even include commercial appliances. The cabinets in the contemporary kitchens are either very light wood, painted wood, or more often laminates. The sleek, clean look has made the contemporary kitchen a favorite with a wide variety of people from city apartment dwellers to contemporary home residents.

The clean simple lines of a contemporary kitchen increase the illusion of space. Light walls and cabinets typical of this type of kitchen also help to give a larger appearance. Glass cabinet doors are often combined with solid door fronts for a more open feeling.

In this age of high-tech, however, the state-of-the-art kitchen does not have to incorporate a stark

*Alno's Alntoun natural spruce kitchen creates a cozy atmosphere with rustic panelled cabinet doors.
Photo courtesy of Alno Kitchen Cabinets, Inc.*

look. The modern kitchen with clean lines, sharp angles, and hard materials can achieve a warmth and softness through the use of different woods and soft colors.

WHITE KITCHEN

Disregarded as a decorating theme for the last two decades, the all white kitchen is making a comeback in conjunction with European styling. The appeal of white is timeless. A white kitchen is like a basic black dress. Like the dress it too can be dressed up or down with additional colors and accessories.

If the kitchen has white cabinets, then the floor, counter, and wall colors can be as dramatic or soothing as the cook desires. White cabinets can either be lacquered wood or laminates. Strong colors in solid surface, laminate, or tile countertops can make a dramatic statement. White cabinets can be topped with black granite countertops for a stunning effect.

The use of one color as an accent on cabinet handles, trims, and sink can make a very dramatic statement in an all-white kitchen. Red for instance, can brighten the kitchen and make it a fun place in which to work. Any accent color can be used, provided it is a strong tone. The strong colors of red and black can be successfully combined as an accent to a white kitchen. In one red and white kitchen, designed by Marilyn Atkins, ASID, for the Kohler Design Center, a checkerboard design on the floor was repeated in the backsplash of the countertops.

There is a renewed interest in the lightness and cleanliness white can give. Polished brass hardware and accessories can add a touch of warmth to this type of decor. On the other hand, polished chrome handles and accent edgings can further emphasize a sleek European look. To conform to the new white trend in kitchen decor, many appliance manufacturers are offering their appliances in either white to blend with the decor or black for a sharp contrast.

Although white can give a stark feeling — the hospital look — to a room, it is the most versatile of colors. It can brighten and expand the look of almost any kitchen. Painted white walls and cabinets will reflect sunlight from adjacent windows and create a cheery kitchen. Color can be added in the form of accents or accessories to fit your mood or the season.

Warm woods can be paired with a basically white kitchen as accent strips on cabinets, butcher block countertops, or in flooring.

COUNTRY KITCHENS

A continually favorite style of kitchen is the country kitchen. Its warm, friendly atmosphere abounds with wood, collectibles, and suggests lots of activity. The wood tones used in today's country kitchen vary from traditional dark tones to lighter stains. The country kitchen is often combined with a dining area or family room.

The term country kitchen today has different meanings. A country kitchen may refer to a very rustic looking one with hand-pegged cabinets in pickled or distressed wood, plank flooring, exposed beams, and tile, maple, or butcher block countertops. Tinware, brass, and copper provide good accents. On the other hand, the term country kitchen may refer to a high-tech kitchen with sculptured warm wood cabinets, tile floor, and tile countertops. There are also many examples that would fit between these two descriptions. However, regardless of the exact meaning, the country kitchen should blend old-fashioned comfort with up-to-the-minute cooking equipment.

Many people want or have a country kitchen and they usually coordinate it with the decorating style of the rest of the house, which many times is situated in a rural atmosphere. However, a kitchen can be decorated in country style in an apartment in a large city. It just needs the right atmosphere and sufficient space to accommodate bulkier looking cabinets and accessories, and to create a backdrop for antiques which can add an air of elegance.

Red accents and checkerboard pattern give this kitchen a very cheerful look. Designed by Marilyn Atkins, ASID for the Kohler Design Center. The white cabinetry and countertop are accented by Kohler's Black Black™ Lakefield™ kitchen sink with a Flair II™ faucet in polished chrome. Photo courtesy of Kohler Co.

Alno's Alnochrome kitchen features delicate chrome handles as well as chrome edging strips. Photo courtesy of Alno Kitchen Cabinets, Inc.

Country kitchens are cozy and often include antique pieces of furniture, antique kitchen appliances, or collections of cherished items of pottery, tinware, baskets, or copperware. Cabinet doors can be of the raised or recessed panel variety. These kitchens are a mixture of natural materials such as wood, brick, tile, marble, granite, and even plaster. Wallpaper is often used as an accent. Storage facilities in this type of kitchen can be varied and include manufactured cabinets as well as free-standing pieces of furniture such as a cupboard or dry sink.

Many of the items used in everyday cooking are in full sight or on display instead of being hidden behind sterile cabinet doors. Storage is attractive to the eye and varied in open cupboards, on shelves, hung on racks on the wall, or in attractive canisters. Plate racks might hold everyday dinnerware.

Many cabinet manufacturers offer the country look in their cabinet designs. Some have open storage units as well as glass-fronted wall cabinets, which can be used to display your favorite dinnerware, glasses, or serving pieces.

Even with today's high-tech appliances, a kitchen can have country charm with cabinets and other decorations. However, reproductions of old ranges equipped with modern features are available. Hoods for ventilation can have a country atmosphere with the use of brass, copper, or wood or they can even be built into a brick wall. Lacking a ventilation hood, many country kitchens have a pot rack over a center island. It makes an eye-catching display even if the pots are never used. A double white enameled sink with brass fittings would further enhance the country theme.

Included in the term country kitchen is its close cousin the colonial kitchen, which often has wallpaper, a fireplace in the family area, and colonial style table and chairs for dining.

The Shaker kitchen, also influenced by our past history, has an unadorned efficient look with wood cabinets of simple lines, lending warmth to the kitchen. Its unadorned style of straight cabinet doors has influenced many cabinet manufacturers. They have either reproduced the true Shaker style in their cabinets or added some beading to the doors of the cabinets. This type of decor makes a very clean, warm looking kitchen in either stained or painted wood cabinets and coordinates well with a traditional home.

PROVINCIAL AND COUNTRY EUROPEAN

The provincial kitchen, as far as today's manufacturers are concerned, is somewhat more formal than the strict country kitchen. Rather than raised panels on cabinet doors, a decorative beading is offered, which can be the same color as the cabinets or a contrasting one. Most people today regard the provincial style of decor as country French with accents of blues, yellows, and soft reds.

Country European also has a French influence and sets a cheerful, informal mood. The style combines graceful arches, open shelving, and intricate trims. In this type of kitchen cabinetry there is great attention to detail. It is an informal look with a casual atmosphere. The woods used can either be light such as oak or dark such as cherry or mahogany. Ceramic tile, wallpaper, and wood are generously used throughout these styles of kitchens. However, it is a neat look, not a cluttered one.

THEME KITCHENS

A kitchen's style of decoration can also be determined by a theme which is either an interest of its owner or is associated with the area where the home is located.

The Southwestern part of our nation has spawned a style of decor not only for kitchens but for entire homes. This style of kitchen incorporates colors inspired by the desert and creates a mellow mood. Adobe bricks, quarry tile, copper, rough plaster, and wood are the primary materials of a Southwestern kitchen.

Wood-Mode's country kitchen in the Hallmark collection features raised panel cabinet doors, quarry tile floor, ceramic tile countertops, a shelf for collectibles above the window, and a traditional dining table and chairs. The skylight provides extra natural light. Photo courtesy of Wood-Mode.

Wood-Mode's Provincial frameless cabinets are a modern translation of French provincial motifs. Photo courtesy of Wood-Mode.

Quaker Maid's Country Traditions custom kitchen in oak with Antique Frost finish and traditional style cabinets. Arched valances and decorative cutouts adorn the open shelves. Photo courtesy of Quaker Maid.

Kitchen collectibles can create a theme for decorating. For example, kitchen advertising art can enhance the walls; old tin graters can be hung, as can baskets made either of natural fibers or wire; old copper and tin pots can be hung above an island cooktop; and antique coffee, chocolate, tea, or cracker tins can be placed on a prominent open shelf in the kitchen. The old and the new can easily be combined in a kitchen. For instance, cast iron pans can hang in harmony with track lighting in a kitchen that ties the past and present together.

You can also decorate your kitchen with the theme of your favorite cuisine. French or Italian cooking accessories, utensils, pottery, and china can provide a warm atmosphere and enhance your cooking at the same time. You might also want to display some of the cooking condiments that do not require refrigeration.

An interest in travel often spawns a collection of posters, drawings, or paintings of your favorite area. These are very compatible with a contemporary kitchen design.

THE SMALL KITCHEN

A small kitchen often presents decorating problems. Although compact, with all of the necessary equipment, it usually seems crowded. You can, however, decorate a small kitchen to make it appear larger.

Light walls and cabinet colors will give a larger appearance. Clean and simple lines as well as some curved surfaces will increase the illusion of space. A mirrored backsplash behind a corner sink, which is quite common in small kitchens, makes the corner seem roomier. Glass doors on some of the upper cabinets can also give the illusion of space. With a wide frame around the glass doors, finger-prints will tend not to get on the glass. Opaque glass on doors will still add spaciousness and avoid having to keep the cabinet contents neatly stacked.

Another way to expand your kitchen space is to open it up. Windows and skylights provide extra light and bring the outside in. Removing part of a wall between the kitchen and an adjoining area such as a breakfast room or family room can also create an illusion of space. Even a small odd-shaped opening such as enlarging a conventional door will make a difference.

Many times it is not necessary to remodel a kitchen when with paint, new countertops, and a new floor you can do wonders. You can transform a small kitchen with dark wood cabinets, a dark floor, and dull looking paint into a cheery one with white cabinets, light countertops, and new flooring.

If you want warmth and coolness at the same time in the kitchen, particularly in a smaller kitchen, think about a "pickled" finish or light stain for the wood cabinets. It is a finish that offers richness, but at the same time a sleek sophisticated treatment. Darker cabinets can also be used if there are comparable light areas to balance them.

However, do not be afraid to use some strong colors in a small kitchen. In selecting a color scheme for a small kitchen consider using two complementary colors or even two shades of a single color for the walls and cabinets with an additional contrasting color for accents.

Wallpaper can add a pleasing touch to a small kitchen, however, it should be a small pattern in keeping with the size of the kitchen. A larger, more dramatic pattern could be used on one wall or even the ceiling as long as the colors of the wallpaper are in harmony with the rest of the room.

11
Small Appliances

There is a myriad of small appliances on the market today. The majority of these appliances are electrical, and some of the smaller ones are battery operated. Depending on the appliance, they have features such as variable speeds, delayed time action, or a built-in digital clock. Some of the small appliances are multi-purpose, such as a toaster oven or grill-waffle iron.

Just as in major kitchen appliances and cabinet designs, the emphasis in small appliance design is European styling. Although to me the term European-styling sounds like a campaign slogan or a buzz word of the industry, in reality, it means sleeker looking appliances with rounded corners and at least the illusion of taking up little space — both very American contributions.

I believe that the cooking function of a kitchen could be perfectly well performed using only small appliances. Today you can bake, broil, microwave, convection bake, toast, mix, slice, shred, purée, brew coffee or tea, squeeze juice, make ice cream, make pasta, and bake bread — all with small countertop appliances. Since there is such an array of small appliances, I have focused on only the major ones that are commonly used in cooking and food preparation.

COFFEE MAKERS AND COFFEE GRINDERS

Drip Coffee Makers

The latest innovation in coffee makers by Cuisinart® is truly an engineering feat. You load it with green coffee beans and out comes a perfect cup of coffee. The machine, which looks like a missile on a launch pad, roasts, grinds, and brews in a single unit. The round, elongated cylinder at the top of the machine roasts the coffee beans, anywhere from light to dark roast. The roasted beans then drop to the next level where they are ground. After grinding, the coffee is drip-filter brewed to the strength you have pre-selected.

Coffee tastes are highly individual. What one person regards as a good cup of coffee, others may perceive as muddy or watery. The type of coffee bean used is purely a matter of taste and so is the choice of coffee makers.

The majority of electric coffee makers today use some form of the drip method. Almost every manufacturer of small electric appliances has a drip coffee maker in its line. There are, however, some electric percolators still being manufactured by such firms as Regal and Presto®. These electric percolators make two to twelve cups of coffee and a signal light lets you know the coffee is ready.

In the almost twenty years since electric drip coffee makers were introduced for home use, the basic technology behind the "perfect cup of coffee" has not changed. Like the first Mr. Coffee, the machines on the market today still heat a pre-measured amount of water to about 200 degrees F. After the water is heated, it still drips through a filter basket filled with ground coffee into a carafe that sits on top of a warming plate. The majority of electric coffee makers today use some form of this drip method.

When purchasing an electric coffee maker, most of us are interested in which model will require the least amount of work to produce a decent cup of coffee. Most of the electric coffee makers use the same brewing method, with the difference in the over 100 models on the market today being in the styling and the features.

Several new features have been added to coffee makers. One is the clock-timer which allows the starting time of the coffee to be set up to twenty-four hours in advance. I like that feature because the coffee is ready when we get up in the morning. Black & Decker, Mr. Coffee, Norelco, Braun, Krups, and Proctor-Silex all have this feature. Another advantage to an automatic-timed coffee maker is that it can be filled and set so that the coffee is ready at the right time during a dinner party.

Several of the models also have the ability to turn themselves off after two hours. I think that is a good feature, since it eliminates concern about an appliance being active when you are away from home, if you have forgotten to turn it off. Although some of the models turn themselves off automatically, they can also be switched to stay on until turned off manually.

The coffee makers without timers have to be turned off manually. However, since heat brings out the bitter taste in coffee, it is good practice to drink the coffee a short time after it is made and not let it sit on the hot plate for hours.

Another new and desirable feature of coffee makers is the "brew interrupt," which interrupts the brewing process for twenty to sixty seconds when you pull out the carafe to get a cup of coffee. After the pause, the coffee maker finishes brewing.

Although each coffee maker lists its capacity in cups, there is no standard measurement for these cups. I suggest that you test your own appliance and figure out its capacity according to your coffee cups or mugs.

There are two types of filters in these coffee makers, one shaped like a cupcake and another like a cone. Braun and Norelco have permanent gold metal filters which do not require filter papers.

Krups Coffee Time Plus has advanced programming, Stop 'n Serve, and a touch control panel. Photo courtesy of Robert Krups North America.

However, we have found that clean-up is much easier with our Braun when we use a paper filter.

Some of the other features of coffee makers are cord storage, a cover for the carafe, and a lid on the water reservoir. Many coffee makers have unique features all their own, such as a water reservoir which can be carried to the sink, adjustable controls that let you dial the strength of your coffee, variations in brewing amounts from half to full capacity, and a thermal carafe. Many manufacturers, such as Braun and Krups, have slick European designs for their coffee makers.

How many times have you broken the carafe of the coffee maker? We have done it several times and then had to write the manufacturer to get another one. In between the breaking of the old one and the arrival of the new one, instant coffee did not taste right. Proctor-Silex has developed a more rugged carafe made of polypropylene for its "Sentry" Coffee Maker to reduce the possibility of breakage. The insulated double wall construction of this carafe keeps the coffee hot throughout the brewing process and up to two hours after brewing has finished. The filter basket of this coffee maker is also insulated to minimize heat loss during brewing.

Some Melitta, Proctor-Silex, and Bosch models can be used to brew tea as well as coffee. Braun has a new plastic tea filter for their wide array of Aromaster coffee makers. The clear plastic tea filter replaces the filter in the Braun coffee maker. Up to six cups of tea can be steeped for the desired length of time and then passed into the preheated carafe by manually turning the flow-through valve. This patented attachment can hold either loose tea leaves or tea bags.

Espresso Makers

A good cup of espresso should be dark in color, have full flavor, and be covered with a layer of thick foam. To produce good results an espresso machine must be able to heat water to approximately 200 degrees F. and have sufficient pressure to force the water and steam through the ground beans quickly.

There are three major types of espresso machines — stove-top, steam, and pump. These machines range in price from about $12 for the simplest stove-top model to $800 for the most powerful pump type.

The pump machines are the most powerful and produce the finest aromatic cup of espresso. The pump machine also produces considerable foam on top since the water is forced through finely-ground coffee at a fast rate. Some of these machines have a 3-quart water reservoir, which is ideal for parties when you want to serve a number of cups of espresso. This eliminates having to refill the water reservoir and waiting for the water to

heat. With smaller machines only one or two cups can be made at a time before the water has to be replaced. The pump type of machines tend to be rather large and some may be noisy.

In the steam machines, steam pressure and gravity work together to move the water through the ground coffee, resulting in an espresso with little foam. According to some studies, the Salton™ Three-For-All™ machine, a steam machine, makes good espresso as well as cappuccino and regular drip coffee. It is one of the most reasonably priced machines of its kind on the market.

Steam machines usually produce from two to nine demitasse cups of espresso as well as a moderate amount of steam for frothing milk for cappuccino. (Cappuccino is espresso coffee topped with frothed hot milk and a sprinkling of cinnamon.) In most cases you brew all of the coffee at once and while it is brewing you can steam the milk if you are making cappuccino. There is also a separate cappuccino frothing machine available.

Not only is there a difference in espresso machines, but there is also a difference in the type of coffee used in these machines. The pump machine uses a very fine espresso grind which is packed down in the brewing basket so that the highly pressurized water will quickly become infused with the coffee as it passes through. The steam machine uses a slightly coarser grind of coffee which should not be packed down since this would slow the gravity flow of the water. While the pump machine requires that you buy specially packaged coffee, you can grind your own for the steam machine.

The stove-top machine, which is the least expensive, brews espresso on your cooktop. It is compact and lightweight, and works on the same principle as the steam machine.

Coffee Grinders

Our grandmothers used to grind coffee beans manually in a coffee mill. Today we either purchase ground coffee or use a small electric appliance to

Braun's espresso machines – the steam machine on the right and the pump machine on the left. Photo courtesy of Braun, Inc.

Salton's Three-For-All™ makes drip coffee, espresso, and cappuccino. The unit has a removable nozzle steam jet for cappuccino. Photo courtesy of Salton/Maxim Housewares Group.

grind it. However, there are still some manually operated coffee mills on the market.

There are two types of electric appliance that grind coffee — a coffee mill and a coffee grinder. The coffee mill is a much larger appliance and operates on the same principle as a grain mill. It grinds the coffee beans between two milling disks – one stationary and one rotating. The fineness of the coffee is determined by how close the disks are set. Bosch's "Columbia" Coffee Grinder has thirty-three settings for the exact grind you desire. The dial on the grinder can be set for the number of cups you plan to brew, thus grinding only the coffee you need.

The coffee grinder chops the beans with two metal blades attached to a central stem, like a blender or food processor. The ground or semi-ground beans whirl around until the desired grind is achieved. Coffee aficionados prefer the more expensive coffee mill, claiming it yields a more delicate cup of coffee. I cannot tell the difference.

COOKING APPLIANCES

Slow Cookers

Slow cookers, known as crockpots, have again become fashionable in recent years because the working woman can start a meal, go to work, and come home to a dish that is ready to serve. Crockpots of various shapes and sizes were the rage in the 1960s and have again become a well used kitchen appliance with over three million sold last year.

The slow cooker operates on the same principle as slow cooking in a pot on top of the stove. A lid covers the pot during cooking, retaining the heat. Hot food usually produces steam, which rises to the top of the pot and collects on the underside of the lid. The steam falls back onto the food in the form of liquid and bastes the food as it slowly cooks. Food in slow cookers is generally cooked at 160 degrees F. which is sufficient to kill any bacterial growth. Since these cookers are covered they are

Braun's coffee grinder has easy to read measuring lid. Photo courtesy of Braun, Inc.

able to retain a steady heat. As a general rule, it takes seven to ten hours to cook meat and vegetables on a low setting.

Each of the slow cookers on the market has unique features of its own. For example, Hamilton Beach has an Automatic Temperature Shift on some of their slow cookers. This enables you to set the cooker for high temperature for 1¾ hours, after which the unit shifts automatically to low for the remainder of the cooking time. The cooker also has manual high and low settings.

Many slow cookers are available with a removable crock or casserole that can be used on the stove top to brown meat before slow cooking it. Rival, which has the patented name Crock-Pot, uses a Corning Ware insert as its casserole which can go from freezer to oven, microwave, or stove top. Presto's® slow cooker has a crockery insert. West Bend has non-stick aluminum casseroles that can be used on the stove top. Without the casserole insert, the West Bend base can be used as a griddle or as a food warmer.

Deep-Fryers

Using deep-fryers used to frighten people, because their use was frequently related to kitchen fires; they smelled up the kitchen when they were used; and they were generally messy to clean. Fear no more, there is a whole new generation of deep-fryers for today's cooks.

The single most important feature of the new deep-fryers is safety. In most of the models the frying is done with the lid of the appliance closed. The food can be seen through a tempered glass viewing window in the lid. Many of the deep-fryers have a charcoal filter in the lid which screens out odors. For safety, the fry basket's raising and lowering controls are on the outside of the deep-fryer. After the oil has reached the desired temperature, you simply open the lid, place the basket of food into position on the control handle, close the lid, and lower the food into the hot oil via a control device on the outside. Cooking takes place with the cover closed, so that there are no grease spatters as the food is frying. On most deep-fryers there is a preset thermostat to control the frying temperature.

The oil capacity and consequently the food capacity varies according to the deep-fryer. For instance, the Salton™ and Tefal deep fryers have a capacity ten cups of oil, while the DeLonghi holds four cups.

However, the DeLonghi Roto-Fryer's unique feature is that the frying basket revolves on a tilted, motorized axis. Food is not submerged in oil but instead rotates in and out of the hot oil, resulting in, DeLonghi claims, evenly cooked, non-greasy food. Since the food goes in and out of the oil during cooking, 50% less oil is used.

In most of the fryers, the basket and lid components are dishwasher safe. The fryer itself can be cleaned with hot soapy water.

Many manufacturers produce various sizes of deep-fryers and some of them can also be used as slow cooker or steamers.

Toasters

Toasters of one form or another go back to colonial days, when slices of bread were placed in a rack before the open fire. First one side of the bread was toasted and then the other. When the cookstove was introduced in the mid 1800s, the cooktop with a holder for bread became the toasting surface. An electric toaster was developed around the time of World War I, but it still required toasting one side at a time with manual turning. In 1926 Toastmaster designed the first pop-up toaster.

I doubt whether any cook today could prepare breakfast day in and day out without a toaster or a toaster oven. There is now a wide variety of toasters on the market. They come in one, two, and four slot models. Their appearance varies from sleek-looking white, black, or pastel models to replicas of cumbersome units of forty years ago. Sunbeam's Radiant Control Toaster, however, is not a replica; it is the same toaster the company first introduced in 1949 and has produced ever since.

Proctor-Silex, producers of toasters since 1928, has a reproduction of its Classic Toaster fitted with today's technology. "Many people want a traditional look in their appliances," said Judy McBee, executive vice-president of marketing for Proctor-Silex. The Art Deco look of this toaster comes from chrome finishing and detail work on the end panels, which are die-cast for durability. Inside the Classic Toaster is modern technology including wide slots for toasting a variety of breads and instant reset which makes consecutive toasting faster. The toaster also has a special setting for defrosting frozen breads and pastries.

One of the features of today's toasters is a rack that automatically lowers itself when the bread is placed on it. Another modern feature is wide slots, especially designed for uncut bagels or English muffins. On many wide slot toasters the racks adjust to the width of the food by moving inward when the rack is lowered. This action centers the bread between the heating elements. Tefal makes a Thick'N Thin Toaster with one of the long slots for thin bread, the other for thicker, allowing you to toast a bagel in one slot and a slice of bread in the other.

In this new technological age there are toasters that are controlled by a microchip rather than a thermostat. The microchip senses the heat of both the food and the toaster. This type of toaster is designed to keep the toasting temperature uniform when many consecutive batches of toast are made. Toastmaster's Master Mind™ heat/moisture sensor goes even further by automatically compensating for the degree of bread freshness to give you the same color toast every time.

Most of the new toasters have double wall construction, which means that while they are warm to the touch they will not burn your fingers. The manufacturers' term for these toasters is "cool to the touch."

Many of the toasters, such as the Moulinex models, have the "keep warm" feature. Some of the long slot models have a built-in rack above the toast slot to warm rolls, pastries, and muffins. All toasters have crumb trays for easy cleaning.

Toastmaster makes a four-slice toaster that is mounted under a wall cabinet. You open the door and put the bread into four slots for toasting. This toaster has an automatic shut-off at the end of the toast cycle with an audible signal. The unit adjusts to accommodate different cabinet styles and the front trim panel protects cabinets from heat and moisture.

The "Flip-Over" by Tefal is more than a toaster. In its vertical position it is a thick and thin toaster accommodating various widths of baked goods. With a quick flip to its horizontal position the appliance becomes a mini oven in which a dual heating system cooks food from below and above. There are two positions for the baking tray to allow for either baking or top browning.

One of the newest appliances for breakfast preparation is the Fresh Express Oven, which looks similar to a toaster but does much more. It has a lift-

DeLonghi Roto-Fryer uses 50% less oil and circulates the food in and out of the oil while frying. Photo courtesy of DeLonghi America, Inc.

Krups' Toastronic I toaster has an extra wide, long slot. A microchip monitor ensures uniform toasting automatically. Photo courtesy of Robert Krups North America.

Proctor-Silex Classic Toaster — a combination of yesterday's traditional design with today's technology. Photo courtesy of Proctor-Silex, Inc.

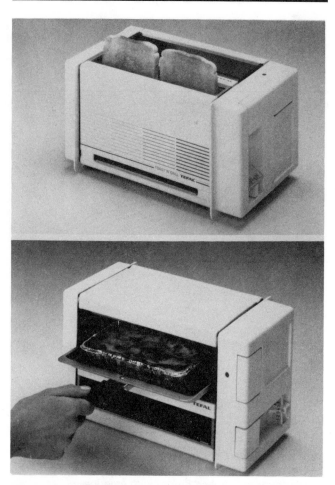

Tefal's Flip-Over Toast and Grill is a wide slot toaster when placed vertically and a mini-oven when placed horizontally. Photo courtesy of T-Fal Corporation.

up cover under which are six wide slots for cooking. You can pour batter into each of the six slots to make pancakes, muffins, omelets, cornbread, or even chicken patties. The unit will also toast four pieces of English muffins and prepare two eggs at the same time. That way you can make McMuffins™ at home.

Another new type of toaster is the Hot Diggity Dogger, which prepares 2 wieners and 2 buns simultaneously. The buns are heated at a different temperature to stay crunchy while the hot dog is cooked just the way you like it with the variable heat control. The wiener basket is removable for easy cleaning and there is a crumb tray.

Toaster Ovens

There is a wide range of toaster ovens on the market. They are a multi-purpose appliance since they are full-size toasters, as well as miniature ovens and broilers.

Sometimes a toaster oven is all the oven you need, particularly on a hot day when you are baking a small casserole and do not want to heat up the kitchen with the big oven. They also come in handy when heating a small amount of food or making one or two grilled sandwiches.

There is one caution to be observed with toaster ovens. Their tops and sides tend to heat up and consequently should not be touched when the oven is on. Although some units are available with "keep-cool" sides, they still do warm up. Some of the models have a slide-out toasting rack that pulls out when the door is opened.

Some models of toaster ovens have a thermostatically operated light that indicates when the oven has reached the desired temperature. The Panasonic has a built-in timer and a preheat switch.

The Sanyo toaster oven is a most unusual model because it is bi-level. It is vertical with two shelves for toasting or baking and takes up less counter space than the average toaster oven. The Proctor-Silex models of toaster ovens have a two-way adjustable rack plus a flip-over broiling pan and claim to have 40% more capacity than other ovens.

Many of the toaster ovens have a continuous clean cycle so that any spills will burn off during use.

Both the Black & Decker Spacemaker and the West Bend Oven-up come with mounting shelves enabling you to mount them under wall cabinets, saving space on kitchen counters.

Proctor-Silex Ovenmaster Toaster Oven has a two-way adjustable rack and is large enough for a 10-inch tart or a 5-pound chicken. Photo courtesy of Proctor-Silex, Inc.

Regal's Griller is portable and convenient for year round grilling. Photo courtesy of Regal Ware Inc.

Countertop Ovens

For small amounts of baking and broiling there are a variety of ovens that bake and broil and sit on the countertop, although they cannot be used as toasters. Many are large enough to hold a roast, a 10-pound turkey, or a 10½-inch pizza. The interior has two racks and most are continuous cleaning.

The countertop oven, however, has the advantage of having more capacity than a toaster oven and can act as a second oven if there is only one built-in oven. The disadvantage is that this oven takes up approximately 20 inches of counter space. If you are contemplating buying a countertop oven and need to place it under a wall cabinet, make sure it will fit with sufficient room for air circulation.

Convection Ovens

Countertop ovens which bake by convection heat only are available from several manufacturers, such as Farberware and Toastmaster. (For explanation of convection baking, see Chapter 5.)

The Toastmaster convection oven has three

cooking systems — convection baking and roasting, broiling and slow cook, plus dehydrating. The dehydration racks are optional.

Microwave Ovens

There are many portable microwave ovens on the market today. Some are a combination microwave-convection oven. (See Chapter 5 for a discussion of microwave and convection ovens.) Many of the portable microwave ovens have electronic touch controls with such features as automatic defrost, three stage programmable cooking, delay start, and a turntable for even cooking.

Even though microwave ovens have been on the market for over fifteen years, new innovations are still being developed. For instance, Sunbeam makes an Express Oven, which is a combination toaster, broiler, and microwave oven. It is ideal for reheating or defrosting meals. Toshiba has developed the first microwave oven with a three dimensional turntable. Not only does the turntable go around, but it also moves up and down creating a spin wave effect. The manufacturer claims that this provides better cooking by placing the food in different microwave energy fields.

Indoor Grills

Smokeless indoor grills have been developed which are portable and convenient to use year around. They can be used for almost every type of meal from grilled sandwiches to steaks and chicken.

Most of the units have two heating positions achieved by rotating the position of the grill rack. Fats from cooking drop to a water-filled tray which is easy to clean. Indoor grills are also available with kabob holders.

Tefal's indoor barbecue grill broils on top and underneath at the same time using one heating element. It also comes with kabob holders so that you can grill kabobs and broil hamburgers at the same time. The unit is virtually smoke-free, so the manufacturer claims.

Electric Frying Pans

Electric frying pans, like many small electric appliances, have become household standards. They are available in various sizes; most have a non-stick finish and a full range adjustable temperature control. When the control is removed from the pan, it is completely submersible for easy cleaning.

Presto® has recently added several features to their electric frying pans. New lids of heat-proof materials and larger knobs provide easier handling. A newly designed Control Master® maintains proper cooking temperatures, while the heavy cast aluminum base provides even heating. There is a no-stick coating for easy cleaning.

Electric Wok

Electric woks are used for Oriental stir-frying as well as some deep fat frying. West Bend makes an attractive red or white one which has a full range of temperature control and a non-stick interior finish. Its flat bottom is ideal for quick browning of foods when stir-frying.

Since a wok can produce grease odors, I recommend that it be used under an updraft fan. Generally, the downdraft ventilation systems are not strong enough to remove odors from an elevated stand-alone electric wok.

Jet-Stream Oven

Taking convection cooking a step further is the Jet-Stream Oven from American Harvester. It combines high-speed air flow with controlled temperature to cook three times faster than a conventional oven and two times faster than a convection oven. It cooks foods as quickly as a microwave, but it can also fry, broil, and grill at the same time. This oven, which cooks with a patented "Cyclonic Cooking™" action, can also function as a conventional oven, toaster oven, and rotisserie. By using racks, different types of foods can be cooked at the same time.

The appliance can be expanded through the use of rings to accommodate a 12-pound turkey. All parts except the control arm are dishwasher safe.

Roaster Ovens

Another type of countertop oven is the top-loaded roaster oven. You can cook, steam, bake, roast, and slow cook in one portable unit. The leading manufacturer producing them in a variety of sizes is Nesco.

Since roaster ovens are portable, they are useful for cooking on the patio on hot days. Roaster ovens are also ideal for buffet entertaining and for preparing food ahead. The removable cook-well can be filled with food to be cooked the day before, stored in the refrigerator, and then cooked at party time. With a steam table rack the oven can also be used as a warming unit. There are various racks

Presto®'s 15-inch Jumbo Electric Frying Pan accommodates a large roast. Photo courtesy of National Presto Industries, Inc.

Jet-Stream Oven by American Harvester cooks as fast as a microwave oven, yet has the ability to fry, boil, and grill at the same time. Photo courtesy of American Harvester.

available for versatile placement of cooking utensils so that you can cook multiple foods at the same time.

Roaster ovens have a full range of temperature controls for baking, roasting, and cooking.

Waffle Makers

Waffles are made from a batter — usually milk, eggs, shortening, flour, and baking powder — that is baked on a grid-shaped griddle. When baked and served, the upper part of the waffle remains crisp, while the lower grooves absorb whatever is put on the waffle — syrup, butter, whipped cream. Waffles are not restricted to breakfast food, but they can be served for lunch topped with a saucy mixture of vegetables or meat; or for dessert, topped with ice cream or whipped cream and fresh fruit.

Waffle makers come in two sizes of grids and have various features. One grid makes Belgian waf-

fles, which are thicker and have deeper grooves, and the other makes traditional waffles. The grids on most of the waffle makers have a non-stick coating, making the removal of waffles easier. The units also have an off light that indicates when the waffle iron is preheated and ready to use.

The size of waffles varies with each manufacturers' product. Many have a square grill that makes one large waffle that breaks into four smaller squares. There are also round waffle makers that make one large waffle which can be broken into four parts. The Rival waffle maker has two rectangular grills which produce two waffles.

Most of the waffle makers have snap out grills that can be washed and put back into place. On some of the waffle makers the grills are reversible — one side for waffles and the other for grilling sandwiches, or cooking bacon and eggs. Rival's Around-the-Clock Baker also has a shallow snap-in grill plate that makes pizzelles, very thin cookies.

Waffle makers are available in chrome or in pastel enameled colors.

Bread Machines

With a bread machine all that is necessary for a perfect loaf of bread are the ingredients and the time for the machine to work. The machine handles it all — the mixing, the kneading, the first and second rising, and the baking. The size of the loaf and the time it takes to produce it vary with each machine. Most machines produces a 1-pound or 1½-pound loaf and require about four hours to do so. However, the Bread Maker by Welbilt takes only 2¼ hours and the National Bread Baker takes 2¾ hours.

All of the machines are able to bake various types of bread, depending on the ingredients you choose. You can add raisins, nuts, pieces of pumpkin, and different grains. Some of the bread makers can be programmed to stop operation after the first rising, so that you may take the dough out and shape such items as French bread, dinner rolls, doughnuts, pizza dough, and croissants, and then proceed to let them rise again and bake them in a conventional oven.

Another feature of the bread machines is delayed bake, which lets you program when the machine should start. This is a nice feature if you want fresh bread for breakfast. Microcomputers control the operation of these machines and many of them have a convection cool-down cycle so that the bread does not have to be removed from the oven immediately when it has finished baking. On some bread makers such as the one by Cuisinart® you can also select the type of crust you desire — normal, thick, or thin; the size of loaf — large or small; and the baking time — regular or speedy.

Indicator lights on the Hitachi Home Bakery let you know which stage of the bread making is currently being performed. The machine also has a room temperature sensor and a dough sensor to provide the perfect temperature control for dough rising. The bread is baked by convection heat and is also cooled by convection.

Cuisinart® Bread Maker allows you to program the type of crust and size of loaf. Photo courtesy of Cuisinarts, Inc.

The non-stick coating on the bread pan lets the bread slide out easily and eliminates messy clean-ups.

Food/Rice Steamers

Probably a Japanese innovation, the food/rice steamer is not only ideal for rice cooking but also steams vegetables, meat, poultry, and even desserts. Hitachi is one of the leading manufacturers of this type of steamer and makes three models in various sizes. The units all have an insert tray for steaming, along with a measuring cup for rice.

When using the steamer as a rice cooker, it not only cooks the rice but keeps it at proper serving temperature for up to four hours.

Zojirushi, another Japanese manufacturer, produces separate rice cookers and separate steamers. The rice cookers have built-in heat sensors that regulate the power supply, allowing the cooker to adapt to a variety of ingredients such as brown rice, sweet rice, rice porridge, and regular rice. The cookers can also be programmed for various types of foods.

Zojirushi rice cookers and food cookers. Photo courtesy of Zojirushi America Corporation.

FOOD PREPARATION APPLIANCES

Hand-held Mixers

Our grandmothers beat egg whites with a wire whisk and cake batter with a spoon. Today we have all types of electric and battery operated mixers to beat anything in a recipe which calls for the slightest agitation.

A hand-held mixer does not take the place of a powerful stand mixer, which is used for big cakes and other large projects. The hand mixer comes in handy when you want to whip a couple of egg whites or a little whipped cream to top a dessert, make a sauce, or mix light to medium batters. However, many of the newer models are powerful enough to mix heavy cookie doughs.

All hand-held mixers used to look alike, but today many have unique features all of their own. The strength of the motors varies in hand-held mixers. The standard motors are rated at 100 watts. The higher-powered mixers, of course, offer more power and more control. For example, Regal's Variable Speed Electronic Hand Mixer is rated at 130 watts and has variable speeds which can be increased or decreased with a smooth operation.

Sunbeam's Professional Mixmaster® Hand Mixer rated at 175 watts has large beaters, five speeds, and a ''burst of power'' button that provides extra mixing power.

Sunbeam's new hand-held electronic Mixmaster® instantly adapts power and speed to prevent bogging down in heavy batters or racing when mixing light mixtures. The two beaters of the electronic Mixmaster® hand mixer are in line rather than side by side, making a sleeker looking unit and one that is easier to store. Also included with the mixer are a whisk, a plastic stir paddle, and a chrome-plated blender rod.

A similar electronic mixing sensor is built into KitchenAid's new Ultra Power Plus Hand Mixer. This mixer was also one of the first to eliminate the center post on its beaters, which helps eliminate clogging and food collection. Bosch's hand mixer also has the open design and comes with a pair of dough hooks. In Toastmaster's hand mixers, the beaters are stored on a clip on each side of the mixer.

Before purchasing any hand-held mixer, make sure it feels comfortable in your hand and is not too heavy for you to hold for a period of time.

Cordless Mixers

The appeal of a cordless mixer is that it is truly portable and can be used anywhere — at the stove, the bar, or even at a campground. Although portable mixers do many mixing tasks well, they are not designed for heavy duty work such as beating a stiff dough. They do many of the smaller tasks, such as whipping a small batch of egg whites or cream, blending salad dressings, and making light doughs.

Portable mixers are rechargeable and charging time varies from one to twenty-four hours. Each charge is good for about thirty minutes of continuous use. Many of the models can either be set on the counter, in a cabinet, or mounted on the wall, with the attachments either standing or hanging.

Many of the portable mixers have variable speeds. For example, the Proctor-Silex Whipper

KitchenAid Ultra Power Plus Hand Mixer with five-speed control, electronic mixing sensor, Turbo Beater™, and easy clean design. Photo courtesy of KitchenAid.

Braun Immersion Blender not only purées and blends, but also chops. Photo courtesy of Braun, Inc.

Snapper™ has three speeds. Some of the portable mixers come with various attachments, such as a plastic or nylon beater for nonstick cookware. Other attachments include wire balloon whisks for adding air to whipped mixtures, spiral whisks for flat bottom containers, or a drink stirrer for in-the-glass mixing. The Cuisinart® model has no attachments, but has two beater heads instead of the usual one.

Immersion Blenders

There are several advantages to a hand-held immersion blender. The first being that it can purée a soup in the pan, on the stove. The soup ingredients do not have to be transferred to a blender or food processor and then puréed. They also make a smooth sauce that will stay warm because it was made in the saucepan, and they whip up numerous milkshakes as well as blending a great number of other items.

It is best to use a hand-held immersion blender in a tall narrow saucepan or container to minimize and avoid any splattering.

Several of the immersion blenders have one cutting blade for puréeing and another for whisking or whipping. However, the Waring and Braun immersion blenders only have one blade. A wall mount and a beaker for mixing small quantities is included with most models. Other accessories such as an egg separator and a spatter guard are available with some models. The Krups immersion blender is part of their hand mixer.

Standing Mixers

If you bake a lot of cakes and cookies and knead bread dough, you need a standing mixer. They are more powerful than the hand-held versions and will last a great number of years. Some have more powerful motors and are larger than others. For example, KitchenAid has seven mixers in their line, each having ten speeds, various bowl capacities, and various attachment options. Sunbeam, known for its Mixmaster® line of mixers, has the same number with either nine or twelve speeds.

Most of the stand mixers have one or two bowls on a rotating stand, one or two beaters, and one or two dough hooks. In addition, some models have a paddle beater and a wire whisk.

Oster's Kitchen Center standing mixer includes a blender, a food processor, and slicer-shredder attachments, making it a complete food preparation unit.

Many of today's standing mixers are electronically controlled so that they can adapt to the set speed instantly. Depending on the model, Sunbeam's Mixmasters have either nine or twelve electronically controlled speeds. Several of the Sunbeam models have pictorial control panels.

KitchenAid probably has the widest range of attachments for its various stand mixers. Included with each model is a flat beater for normal to heavy mixing, a dough hook for mixing and kneading yeast doughs, and a wire whip for mixtures that need to incorporate air, such as egg whites and whipped cream. The KitchenAid dough hook is designed with a shield at the top to prevent the dough from climbing up the hook. Some of the optional accessories are a food grinder, pasta maker, sausage stuffer, juice extractor, grain mill, and a two-piece pouring shield.

There are several things to look for when purchasing a stand mixer. The unit should have a sturdy base; the beaters should be able to reach the entire bottom of the bowl; and the beaters and motor housing should be able to tilt back and lock in place so that additional ingredients can be added easily.

Citrus Juicers

Many of us love freshly squeezed orange juice for breakfast, but few of us take the time to make it. Citrus juicers are available in various forms — metal and glass reamers, hand-held wooden reamers, a manual press, and electric citrus juicers. Often, the hand-held wooden reamer does the best job, getting all of the pulp out, and it is an inexpensive kitchen gadget that is good for small jobs. However, to enjoy citrus juice in large quantities, an electric citrus juicer saves a lot of time and effort.

Some of the electric citrus juicers come with two cones, one for small fruit and the other for large fruit such as grapefruit. On some models the direction can be reversed by simply lifting the fruit and starting the juicing process again. This helps eliminate clogging, and reversing the action results in more juice. Some models have containers to hold the extracted juice.

Juice Extractors

One of the latest innovations in small appliances is the juice extractor, which lets you extract juice from a great number of fruits and vegetables, such as carrots, beets, celery, spinach, tomatoes, pineapple, bananas, and even potatoes. The juice is extracted from the fruit fibers. Soft fruit such as bananas and peaches will yield a thicker liquid which is more like a nectar.

Juice extractors vary in price, size, and power of their motors. If you plan to use the unit every day then you will want one with a more powerful motor and consequently a more expensive unit than if you were going to use a juice extractor for an occasional glass of carrot juice.

The extraction process varies by model. With some models the vegetables are ground by cutting disks and then the juice is poured out of a spout while the pulp is ejected into another part of the extractor. Other models extract juice by centrifugal force, while still others work like a meat grinder. In the extractors that use centrifugal force, the pulp is collected in a basket. In the grinding types, the pulp remains in the spinning basket while the juice passes through the perforations into a container.

Most juice extractors' parts that come in contact with the fruit or vegetables are made of non-corrosive materials such as stainless steel, plastic, or nylon. Some juice extractors also have the capability to make nut butters and purées, the latter being ideal for baby food.

Tefal's Juice Extractor is two appliances in one. Built with a centrifugal system to extract juices from fruits and vegetables, the unit has an interchangeable citrus juicer attachment that automatically reduces the rotating speed for the squeezing of citrus fruits.

Can Openers

Gone are the days when you had to twist and turn a hand operated device to open a can. Today's electric can openers are available in various shapes and sizes. Many have a scissor and knife sharpener attached. There are also can openers for tall cans, which are designed not to tip over, as well as adjustable can openers whose height can be varied to accommodate tall cans.

Most can openers have magnetic lid holders and automatically stop when the can is opened. Many of the can openers can be mounted on the wall. Some units, like Presto's® Above All™ Can Opener Plus, also open bottles, plastic bags, and jars.

Electric Carving Knife

The electric carving knife makes slicing easier, particularly with a large roast or turkey. Many knives today are operated with rechargeable batteries. All models have stainless steel blades and some have blades that rotate 90 degrees for vertical or horizontal slicing. I am old-fashioned and still like to see my husband manually carve the Thanksgiving turkey or Christmas standing rib roast.

Food Slicers

If you entertain a lot, make a great deal of sandwiches, or are inept at handling a knife, an electric food slicer is for you. Food slicers come in two sizes

Presto®'s Above All Can Opener not only opens cans, but bottles, plastic bags, and jars as well. Photo courtesy of National Presto Industries, Inc.

— large ones that are stationary and smaller ones that fold up for storage. Bosch's "Salzburg" slicer collapses to 3¼ inches for easy storage.

The food slicers produce uniform slices from one-eighth inch to one inch in thickness. Bread, roast beef, turkey breast, cheese, and pickles can all be evenly sliced on a food slicer. For food preparation, apples, potatoes, and even refrigerated cookie dough can be sliced. Almost paper-thin slices of tomatoes can be achieved without squashing them.

Food is placed into the food slicer with one part resting against the metal teeth and the other against the food pusher. As the food is cut the pusher keeps inching the food closer to the slicing teeth. Some slicers have protectors over the teeth which keeps them partially covered during operation. Some models have a switch that can be set for one slice at a time or continuous slicing. On other models you must hold down a button for continuous slicing.

Most models of food slicers can be disassembled completely for easy cleaning and most have a safety lock to guard against accidental use.

Warming Trays

With more hurried and informal lifestyles many company meals are served buffet style. Cooking can be fun and is not that difficult, but sometimes keeping the food hot can be a challenge. For years candle-powered warmers were used for this purpose, but today electric warming trays are more practical and offer a larger warming surface.

Electric warming trays can be very useful for company dinners as well as everyday meals. I have found that an electric warming tray can heat plates for food serving, as well as keep a simple pasta dish warm for second helpings, and keep an entire meal warm for buffet service.

Many models, such as those by Salton™, have a hot spot on their trays. This spot will reach a temperature up to 40 degrees higher than the surrounding surface and makes it a good place to keep coffee, soup, or gravy hot. However, warming trays cannot cook food, they merely keep foods hot with a temperature range from about 150 degrees to 250 degrees F. For optimum efficiency, it is a good idea to preheat the tray before using it. Salton™ also produces a small unit called Jumbo Hot Spot™ which keeps single dishes very hot.

All electric warming trays need to be used near an electrical outlet. However, extension cords can be used. The Cordless Warming Tray from Conair Cuisine operates with a refillable butane chamber, which makes the unit completely portable.

Warming trays are available in several sizes and, depending on the model, with a number of heat adjustments, usually one to four.

West Bend's Buffet Server II will keep a complete entrée hot in its three compartments. The base of 22 by 10 inches can be used as a hot tray or a specially designed stainless steel warming section can be placed on top of the tray. The frame of this section houses two 1½-quart glass warming dishes and a 3-quart stainless steel serving dish. The dishes fit into the frame so that they can be filled and placed in the server. To keep foods hot there is an adjustable control for varying degrees of heat.

Blenders

Blenders were the forerunners of the food processor and still perform some of the functions of the processor. The name Waring is almost synonymous with the whole range of blenders on the market. As their name implies these units are best suited for blending, although they can also purée and chop.

Blenders are available with variable speeds which are usually activated by push buttons. Some units have electronic controls and an on/off pulse action. A removable cap at the top of the 40-ounce containers lets you add ingredients while blending.

Food Processors

Almost twenty years ago when the first food processor by Cuisinart® was introduced in the United States, it was considered a luxury. Invented by Pierre Verdun, Le Robot Coupe, as the model was named at the time, has revolutionized home food preparation. For the first time, the home cook could not only prepare some of the exotic restaurant dishes but she could also chop, slice, dice, and mix in record time.

Today for many family cooks, the food processor is a necessity and is available in many sizes from mini to compact to full size and almost super capacity. I must admit, I have five food processors — a full size, two compacts, one larger than the other for medium-sized tasks, and two minis. I have relegated one of the minis totally to the task of chopping onions, since I think that no matter how carefully and thoroughly you clean the plastic bowl, it still has a slight odor of onions.

All of the food processors operate in the same manner. There is an electric motor in the base of the unit which turns a central spindle on which a double bladed knife, or a slicing or shredding, disk rotates. This spindle is enclosed in a plastic container with a lid that has an elongated opening, called a feed tube, through which food may be added to the unit or stacked for slicing. The newer food processors such as Braun's Multipractic and the new Cuisinart® also have a whisk attachment, a dough hook, and a kneading attachment, which make the unit a complete food preparation center.

Moulinex has also designed some of their food processors to be complete kitchen machines. For example, their Delux Kitchen Machine is not only a food processor, but also has a blender attachment as well as a juice extractor and citrus juicer. The food processor of the unit includes a chopping blade, a dough blade, two reversible discs for slicing and grating, a masher/purée accessory, a French fry disc, an emulsifier disc, and a separate mini chopper.

Regal's compactly styled Processor Plus includes a full size processor and a mini chopper that converts to a coffee and spice grinder. The mini chopper area converts to a coffee grinder with a specially designed "S" blade and heavy duty bowl insert. This exclusive feature means that it is easy to convert from grinding coffee and spices to chopping vegetables without a transfer of hard-to-remove flavors.

Many people have found that the standard size food processor was too large for small tasks, such as making mayonnaise. The compact, sometimes also called mini, food processors are two-thirds to one-half of the size of their big brothers. They all perform the same tasks with powerful motors. Krups' Mini Pro Extra food processor with controlled speed includes two bowls to accommodate recipes that call for more than one chopping or processing step.

Some food processors are available with two bowls, one that does not have a handle, making it awkward to pick up. Several of the lids of the food

processors have small slits in them for adding liquids, such as oil, to the contents of the work bowl. Black & Decker's compact unit, Shortcut, has a different looking blade. It is straight edged on one side and curved on the other so that food cannot get caught under the blades and escape being cut.

Most food processors have an on-off and pulse switch. Braun's food processors have a variable speed control that allows you to control the size of the chopped particles and the thickness of slices as well as variable speeds for different tasks, such as whipping egg whites and cream. Regal's food processor features a precision electronic speed dial for maximum processing control. The Bosch "Strasbourg" processor has three speeds to assure that the right speed is used for each function.

Most food processors come with a chopping blade and a slicing and shredding disk. Depending on the model various other disks are also available, such as a serrated slicing disk, a plastic blade used for doughs, a disk for cutting French-fried potatoes, and the new whisk or mixer disk.

SaladShooter®

Presto's® SaladShooter® is one of the more versatile appliances to enter the food preparation field in recent years. It literally shoots salad ingredients into the bowl. When it originally came on the market it was only electrically operated, but now is also available cordless with a rechargeable power pack.

The SaladShooter® is a slicer and shredder with interchangeable processing cones for slicing and shredding. The food guide pushes the food for continuous operation.

Presto's® new Professional model of the SaladShooter® has four interchangeable cones for thick and thin slices, ripple cuts and shreds, and an expanded chamber to accommodate whole potatoes, zucchini, and cucumbers. All parts of the SaladShooter® are removable for easy clean-up.

Krups' Mini Pro Extra small food processor includes two bowls for more than one chopping or processing task. Photo courtesy of Robert Krups North America.

Regal's food processor with electronic speed dial for maximum processing control. Photo courtesy of Regal Ware, Inc.

Pasta Machines

Pasta machines mix the ingredients for pasta, knead it, and extrude the finished product in about fifteen minutes. The size and shape of the holes in the various discs supplied with the machines determine the shape of the pasta. You can make spaghetti, fettucine, lasagna, and even cookies, bread sticks, and gnocchi with most pasta machines. Most machines make 1½ pounds of pasta.

I have found that letting the pasta dry over a rack or on a cornmeal floured board for several hours results in a less sticky pasta. Electric pasta makers are difficult to clean right after using and it is advisable to let all of the excess dough dry and then gently tap the dried dough from the various parts.

Pasta dough can also be made by hand or in a food processor and then shaped and extruded from a hand-operated pasta machine. Drying also enhances this pasta.

The best known pasta machines are produced by the Italian small appliance manufacturer, Simac and Takka.

OTHER FOOD PREPARATION APPLIANCES

Popcorn Poppers

The most nutritious popcorn is made in a hot air popcorn popper since no oil is used to pop the kernels. Some say that the calories saved by not using oil can be put into the butter to top the popcorn, while others tout unadorned popcorn as a very healthy snack food.

Hot-air poppers pop the corn kernels with electrically heated and driven air. Most of the models have a corn measure and a place to melt butter. You simply pour the corn kernels into the machine, cover it with the lid, and in about four minutes you can have from two to four quarts of popcorn depending on the size of the unit. A few models provide a bowl for the popped corn.

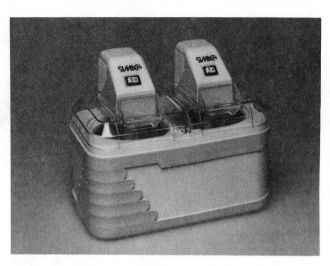

Simac's Il Gelataio Duet ice cream maker can produce two different flavors of ice cream at the same time. Photo courtesy of Simac.

Simac Pastamatic makes all types of pasta from spaghetti to lasagna. Photo courtesy of Simac.

There are also corn poppers available for the microwave oven. Basically they are a bowl with a lid which is filled with a pre-determined amount of corn and placed in the microwave oven on high for three to four minutes. Once you have established the popping time, you can add butter to some of these poppers about one minute before the end of the popping.

Ice Cream Makers and Ice Cream Machines

Ice cream makers, which are not a new innovation, are either manually or electrically operated. Even in colonial America there were hand-cranked ice cream makers. Ice cream machines, which are far more expensive, are refrigerated units that are only operated electrically.

There are basically two types of ice cream makers. The first type, such as Donvier's Premier and Salton's™ Big Chill, have a canister that is placed in the freezer for at least six hours before making ice cream. After removing the canister from the freezer premixed ingredients are added, along with the

mixing blade, the canister is placed in an outer shell, and the unit is stirred manually or electrically for about twenty minutes. The Waring canister is a self contained unit and does not need to be inserted into a housing.

The second type of ice cream makers, such as Waring's Ice Cream Parlor, uses ice cubes and table salt as the chilling agent. You layer the ice cubes and table salt around the filled ice cream canister and plug the machine into an electrical outlet. The canister turns and the ice cream mixture becomes firm in about thirty minutes.

All of these ice cream makers have small holes in the cover to allow for the addition of nuts or other ingredients during the freezing process.

The refrigerated ice cream machines have a built-in cooling system and require no freezing of a canister or the use of ice and salt. The refrigerated units are big, heavy, and are not easily movable. However, the Viva Gelatiera Compact does not quite fit the typical description. It is a smaller, more compact unit and small amounts of water and salt are recommended for perfect operation.

Simac, the Italian appliance manufacturer, was the pioneer in home ice cream machines. The Simac Il Gelataio Super as well as the Gaggia Gelatiera have additional canisters that allow for additional batches of ice cream to be made and frozen. Also the canisters lift out for easy cleaning.

Simac has a new Il Gelataio "Duet" ice cream maker which combines the freezing of the chamber with electrical churning. The entire base, which is divided into two sections for two different ice creams, is first placed in the freezer for a period of time. Then the ingredients are put into each chamber and separate motors are placed on top to churn the ice cream. The motor will automatically reverse direction when the ice cream gets hard and strong resistance is reached. A smaller version of this unit, called Il Gelataio SC, is also available.

All of the ice cream machines are capable of producing a soft or hard ice cream as well as sherbets. The consistency of the ice cream depends on the freezing time.

12
Cooking Equipment

I love my dream kitchen, but I really would not be happy in it unless I had the proper cooking equipment — pots, pans, casseroles, bakers, roaster, baking sheets, cake pans, and the various little tools that make up the spectrum of cooking equipment. We cooks, like fine craftsmen, want the best possible equipment with which to work. We use good, fresh ingredients to prepare our food and we should also use good equipment for its preparation.

COOKWARE

Much of today's cookware has been designed for utmost efficiency as well as ease of use. Over the years new technology has produced new types of cookware. Non-stick finishes have not only cut down on our use of butter and oils, but have made clean-up easier. Freezer-to-oven-to-table cookware has eliminated the need for serving dishes for informal meals.

There is a huge array of cookware on the market today. Since, we all have different styles of cooking it is impossible to evolve the perfect formula of which pieces of cookware are essential to every kitchen. For example, if you use frying pans more than any other cookware you will want them in several different sizes.

BASIC COOKWARE

The number and variety of pieces of cookware depends on your individual style of cooking. If you do a lot of sauce making or steaming of vegetables, you will want several sizes of saucepans. If you cook soups, a stock pot is almost a must, although Dutch ovens can double for soups and stews. Two sizes of frying pans, an 8-inch and a 10-inch, are a must in any selection of cookware. The large one should have a cover so that it can be used for cooking other than frying.

Many selections of cookware are available in sets, which tend to be less expensive than buying the pieces individually. However, the type of pieces in each set varies with the manufacturer. Most 8-piece sets include the following pieces: two saucepans, one smaller that the other, with lids, a covered Dutch oven or larger saucepot, two frying pans, the larger of which can use the lid of the Dutch oven. A set of fairly substantial cookware can be purchased for around $50. However, sometimes it is a good idea to buy just one piece to see if you like the cookware.

The most popular sets of cookware range in price from $50 to $500. An eleven-piece set of Visions by Corning is $55 and an eight-piece set of Revere Ware can be purchased on sale for $50. A fourteen-piece set of Revere Ware not on sale is about $200. Regal's seven-piece enameled drawn aluminum cookware in the Wildflower design is about $75. Farberware, another producer of moderately priced stainless steel cookware, has an eight-piece set for $125. Many of the large chain department stores such as Macy's have their own line of cookware. Macy's Grand Prix stainless steel cookware runs $220 for an eleven-piece set. Circulon has

Wear-Ever®'s new Acclaim® heavy-gauge aluminum fry pans with DuPont SilverStone® Supra interiors. Photo courtesy of Wearever/Member of the Newell Group.

Calphalon®'s anodized aluminum stir-fry pan for stovetop stir-frying. Photo courtesy of Calphalon.

Calphalon® anodized aluminum cookware. Photo courtesy of Calphalon.

Tefal's new Royale Cookware with porcelain exterior. Photo courtesy of T-Fal Corporation.

Regal's enameled drawn aluminum cookware. The seven piece set in the Wildflower design. Photo courtesy of Regal Ware, Inc.

an eight-piece set for $280 and the same number of pieces in Calphalon runs $310. An eleven-piece set of Calphalon is $500. If you like enameled cookware, an eleven-piece set of Chantal is $440 and a seven-piece set of Le Creuset is $375. Many of the sets occasionally are on special promotions or sales.

You can also buy aluminum cookware with a non-stick coating for as low as $3.99 for some pieces in your local supermarket, variety, or junior department store. Although these pieces of cookware may not last as long as the more expensive ones, they are ideal for beginning cooks.

COOKWARE SIZES

Type of Cookware	Sizes
Covered Saucepans	1 quart, 1½ quart, 2 quart, 3 quart, 4 quart
Covered Saucepots	4 quart, 5 quart, 6 quart, 8 quart, also available in 12 quart and 16 quart
Double Boilers	1½ quart, 2 quart
Dutch Oven	5 quart, 6 quart
Stockpots	5 quart, 5½ quart, 8 quart, 9 quart, 12 quart; 18 and 25 quart come with canning lids
Skillets	7 inch, 8 inch, 10 inch, 11 inch, 12 inch, 13 inch; usually the 8, 10, and 12 inch skillets have lids
Covered Frying Pans	7 inch, 8½ inch, 10½ inch, 12 inch (the 12-inch covered frying pans have a helper handle for easy transporting)
Stir Fry Pan	11 inch, 14 inch
Roasting Pans	8½ by 13½ inch, 10 by 16½ inch, 11 by 17 inch, 13½ by 20½ inch

The preceding chart will give you the most popular sizes of various types of cookware. The difference in a Dutch oven and a covered saucepot is that the Dutch oven is deeper and consequently narrower. Skillets are shallower than frying pans and usually do not have a lid. Sizes of cookware vary slightly from manufacturer to manufacturer. Also available from some manufacturers of cookware are a steamer insert and a double boiler insert, converting a saucepan into a steamer or a double boiler. Tea kettles of various sizes and shapes are produced to complement most cookware. With the great interest in stir-fry cooking many manufacturers have added to their line a wok or stir fry pan which can be used on the cooktop.

Cookware Buying Tips

If you are buying new cookware you should first of all determine what type of pan bottom is recommended for use with your cooktop. Then you should carefully inspect the construction of the cookware to see how the handles are attached to the body of the pot or pan. Make certain that the handle, as well as the knob of the lid, is of a material that can safely be put into the oven and dishwasher, if you tend doing so. Also the handle or handles should be comfortable to hold, especially on large pieces that go in and out of the oven. If the handle is of a metal that gets very hot, many of the manufacturers will provide leather sleeves for the handles so that you will not burn your fingers.

Also feel the weight of each individual piece because you do not want it so lightweight that the bottom of the pot or pan will warp after a few uses. On the other hand, you also do not want the cookware so heavy that it is hard to lift. Imagine that 5-quart Dutch oven full of your favorite stew that you have to lift from the cooktop and place in the oven. The pot may feel great empty, but how is it going to feel full of food?

The lid of a pot or pan is also very important. It should fit tightly to hold in the cooking juices, particularly on pots and pans you intend to use for braising and stewing. The lids of many cookwares are tempered glass so that you can see the contents of the pan and check the cooking progress without lifting the lid.

The inside of the cookware is just as important as the outside. In today's world of health consciousness and search for easy care utensils, many pots and pans have a non-stick finish, a stick-resistant finish, or an enamel interior. The enamel interior is also easy to clean, and like the stick-resistant finish requires a little more oil or shortening for cooking.

There are different types of cookware for different cooking tasks. You do not have to have all of your cookware alike. Cast iron, for instance, is good for very high heat retention and for stewing, while aluminum is considered best for steaming by many cooks. I think mixing cookware can give you better overall results than using one specific type.

However, regardless of which type of cookware you might be purchasing, it always takes a little while to get your cooking style adjusted to a new utensil. Some heat up more and others less on the heat setting you have been accustomed to using.

A word of caution, however, before you purchase new cooking equipment. Determine what you are going to replace and if you buy additional equipment to what use you will put it. There is no sense in buying a fish poacher, no matter how pretty it looks, if you never poach fish. However, you may want that pretty copper fish poacher as a collector's piece to display on a kitchen shelf.

Early Cookware

The early settlers of our country used iron pots and pans to cook in the open fireplace. In the early 1800s tin was used to produce some baking utensils and later replaced some of the heavier iron cookware. By the late 1880s lighter weight cast and sheet iron kettles were adopted for use on the cookstove. In the beginning of the 20th century aluminum became the popular cookware and is still being used today in one form or another. Since World War II there have been many technological advances in cookware.

Today we have a variety of cookware from which to choose — cast iron, aluminum, anodized aluminum, copper, stainless steel, a combination of metals, enameled cast iron and other enameled metals, heatproof glass, and ceramic.

Over the years, however, the basic shape of cooking utensils has not drastically changed. They may look a little spiffier, have some technological updates, and take advantage of the new so-called sleek European styling, but they are basically the same shape of pans our mothers and grandmothers used. In this aspect of the dream kitchen, most of us probably do not need to dream; we have reality. Our dreams may be of new cookware with some of the new technological advances, but not basically of new shapes of cookware.

However, it is just not "pots and pans" anymore. Cookware does have a new look. We want several features in cookware — a fashion look for cookware so that we can cook and serve in the same utensil; durability; and non-stick finishes for easy clean-up and healthier cooking.

Aluminum Cookware

Aluminum cookware has been used for almost a century. It is inexpensive, lightweight, and is one of the best conductors of heat. Since it is lightweight, large pots of aluminum can be used to boil pasta, cook soup and other liquid-based dishes, and still be easy to handle.

Over a period of time thin-gauge aluminum pots will tend to warp and thus heat unevenly. Medium and heavy gauge aluminum pots and pans are available from many manufacturers. Another disadvantage to an aluminum pot is that certain acids, like lemon juice, wine, and tomatoes, as well as egg yolks, have a reaction to aluminum. The metal can discolor food and ultimately affect its taste.

That is why today the aluminum cookware on the market has a non-stick coating, such as Silver-Stone® Supra. With the coating and medium to heavy weight aluminum, this cookware has become increasingly popular while still being relatively inexpensive.

Also available are porcelain coated, or clad as the industry calls it, aluminum cookware with a non-stick finish. Regal's present line of Club Cookware, almost a household word for fifty years, is available with this coating in several colors with or without designs.

Today aluminum is also used in cookware as a sandwich for heat conduction with other metals. Aluminum also has been treated or anodized to make it non-reactive.

Anodized Aluminum Cookware

One of the pioneers of anodized cast alloy cookware was John Gordon Rideout, designer of Magnalite Cookware, which first came on the market in 1934. Forty-five years later the General Housewares Corporation, producers of Magnalite, upgraded some of the designs but did not alter the basic concept.

Anodized aluminum cookware consists of aluminum whose surface has been electro-chemically treated to make it non-reactive to foods. The process actually changes the molecular structure of the surface. This type of cookware is fairly heavy and the inside of the pan is stick resistant, but not non-stick. It is advisable to use plastic utensils with these pans, because if the inside surface gets scratched you may get a chemical reaction between the food and the pot.

Most of the anodized aluminum cookware is so efficient that you can reduce your normal cooking temperatures by 25%. Browning takes place on medium instead of medium high.

One of the best examples of anodized aluminum is Calphalon®, a flat-bottomed cookware. The cookware is not cast aluminum but spun or drawn aluminum, which gives it the same thickness all around the pan plus a uniform surface. It has a hard, jewel-like surface achieved after the pan is formed by placing it in an electro-chemical solu-

tion at a controlled temperature. This process changes the molecular structure of the metal, creating a hardness greater than stainless steel and a good-looking gray finish. The resulting cookware has a smooth finish which is non-oxidizing and has a stick resistant surface (not the same as a non-stick surface). With this process there are virtually no hot spots in the bottom of the pan since the heat spreads evenly across the bottom and up the sides of the pan. Riveted cast iron handles make this cookware suitable for all oven and broiler temperatures.

Circulon® is another anodized aluminum cookware which has a unique "Hi-Low" surface of concentric rings on the bottom interior of the pots and pans. These concentric "Hi-Low" grooves are covered with a non-stick coating. It is the variation in the surface that makes this cookware durable.

Cast Iron Cookware

Cast iron is still being used by many cooks, although it is heavy and takes a while to heat up. However, cast iron will get very hot over high heat and brown any food very well. It is the favorite of Paul Prudhomme, the famous New Orleans Cajun cook, who prepares his renowned "blackened fish" in a cast iron skillet. He likes cast iron because it distributes heat well. Cast iron pans also hold heat well.

Cast iron pots and pans need to be seasoned before using and their surfaces should be oiled occasionally to prevent rust. Copco treats the interiors of each piece of its cookware with a durable matte black or white enamel finish to prevent rusting and provide easy cleaning. Most cast iron cooking equipment will last a lifetime. Bob Kellerman, great grandson of the founder of Lodge Iron Manufacturing of Tennessee, said "Cast iron's like a good woman . . . it gets better with age." True, cast iron does not get old, just more seasoned.

Cast iron pots and pans are excellent for slow cooking and for browning. They are ideal for stews, and some of the skillets produce mouth watering cornbread. Cast iron cookware has become very popular for outdoor cookery.

One of the favorite pieces of cast iron cookware is the Dutch oven, which has been used almost since our country began. It is said that the name came from the fact that this piece of cookware, originally called a camp oven, was sold door to door in colonial days by Dutch peddlers.

According to Lodge Manufacturing Company, the most popular pieces of cookware in "Black Iron," as it is called by the aficionados, are a 12-inch skillet, 5-quart Dutch oven, 10½-inch skillet, 10-inch chicken fryer, cornbread skillet, and 7-stick corn-stick pan. Cast iron is also good for griddles. With the great popularity of stir-fry foods, Lodge Manufacturing recently introduced a flat bottom wok/stir-fry skillet of cast iron.

Pierce Arrow, the vintage car company, produces a line of cast iron cookware with porcelain lids that are decorated with a game design.

Ceramic Cookware

Ceramic cookware is among the world's oldest. First made of unglazed clay and then glazed clay, ceramic cookware is still being produced today — many even being made by hand. Ceramic cookware is used for baking, primarily as casseroles with or without lids, open bakers, soufflé dishes, gratin dishes, terrine bakers with or without lids, and shell seafood dishes.

The glaze of ceramic cookware, which is fired at a high temperature, provides a nonporous finish and a smooth surface. However, there are porous ceramic baking dishes on the market, such as the clay baker by Romertopf, which must be soaked in water before using, providing moist baking. High heat, such as 450 to 475 degrees F., is necessary to evaporate the moisture from the vessel, which in turn results in moist cooked food.

Certain glazes, particularly on some non-mass produced ceramic vessels, can contain lead, which could be toxic. Care should be taken to find out what type of glaze was used on any non-commer-

cial cooking ceramics you might buy. If the glaze of the ceramic is lead free, the dish can be used in the microwave oven.

Corning is the best known manufacturer of ceramic cookware. Ceramic cooking vessels can be taken directly from the oven to the table, eliminating the necessity of serving dishes. Corning has recently introduced a new line of Corning Ware® in black. This fluted design brings a dramatic look to the table and can be mixed with the French White Corning Ware® for a stunning effect.

Acroflam, a French cookware manufacturer, produces a ceramic cookware which can be used on the stovetop and in the oven as well as in the microwave. The cookware includes not only casseroles but also pots and pans, which have removable handles for easy storage. Emile Henry's French ceramic cookware has a thinner than usual body and a very smooth interior for easy cleaning.

Combination of Metals in Cookware

Many of today's cookware manufacturers combine the best properties of several metals to produce utensils that will provide optimum cooking efficiency and easy care. For example, copper or aluminum bottoms, which are both excellent heat conductors, are combined with a stainless steel interior and exterior to create an efficient cooking utensil and one that does not react with foods. Cuisine Cookware's Steelpride uses this method and bonds the aluminum bottom to the stainless body.

Sometimes copper or aluminum is used as a core between an outside and inside of stainless steel. Cuisinart®, for example, uses this method of construction in their line of stainless steel pots and pans.

All-Clad Metalcrafters, Inc., makes a variety of combination cookware, all of which is based on a permanent, highly-polished, slick. and corrosion resistant stainless steel interior cooking surface. A thick core of aluminum for even heat distribution is used as the core of each piece of All-Clad cookware. These layers are permanently bonded to an outer layer of either aluminum, copper, or stainless steel, giving you a choice of three cookwares with basically the same cooking properties, but different exteriors.

Copper Cookware

Copper cookware has been the traditional choice of cookware for professional chefs because it responds quickly to changes in cooking temperatures and retains heat well. How many times have you seen a picture of a French chef with beautiful copper cookware and dreamt you had it for your kitchen.

Unfortunately there are several disadvantages to cooper cooking utensils, not the least of which is its price. However, it is not any more pricey than some of the better quality cookware, from both domestic and European manufacturers on the market today. Copper cookware is very heavy to lift and must be cleaned with a special copper cleaner frequently to retain its shiny look. If the copper utensil is lined with tin, it should not be used over very high heat, because the tin may melt.

Castle Copper, an American manufacturer of copper cookware, has lined its copper utensils with a nickel-tin alloy which is harder and more heat conductive than stainless steel. A five-piece set of this cookware is about $300.

Copper is also used for mixing bowls and is excellent for whipping egg whites since the metal interacts with the egg whites to produce a denser and more stable texture.

Copper utensils should never be put into the dishwasher.

Enameled Cast Iron Cookware

Enameled cast iron cookware has a coating of enamel on the outside and may also have it on the inside. The enamel coating on the inside, however, tends to make it more difficult to brown food. The cookware tends to be heavy, but is beautiful in ap-

pearance. The enamel coating on cast iron eliminates the tendency of cast iron to rust. The colorful exteriors of this type of cookware make it ideal for buffet or table service.

One of the best known manufacturers of enameled cast iron cookware is Le Creuset of France. The factory began producing pans in 1925 and still uses the same methods today. The molten cast iron is poured into sand molds by hand where the form is allowed to harden. Each mold is destroyed after its use. The cast iron pans are polished and sanded by hand and then, after passing inspection, are sprayed with two coats of enamel and fired at 1500 degrees F. At this temperature the enamel becomes embodied into the cast iron, resulting in a pot that is resistant to damage.

Le Creuset uses two types of finishes on the interior of their cookware. Their non-stick Castoflon® is a base coat of porous enamel which is coated with SilverStone® (non-stick finish) that is absorbed into the enamel in firing, resulting in a very hard surface. Since Le Creuset cookware has magnetic and heat conduction properties it can be used for induction cooking.

Enameled Other Metal Cookware

Steel is the most popular of the metals to be coated with enamel. However, in order to make this combination a good heat conductor an aluminum sandwich is usually found on the bottom of the pot or pan. This type of cookware is of medium weight and is also very good looking.

Chantal is one of the leading producers of enamel-on-steel cookware. It was founded by German-born Heida Thurlaw who studied engineering. After marrying an American she decided to put her education to work and design cookware for the majority of the people who used it — women, many of whom were working women.

Tempered glass lids that let you view the cooking process are one of the unique features of Chantal enamel-on-steel cookware. Stainless steel handles and knobs are another Thurlaw innovation for

Chantal enamel-on-steel cookware with tempered glass lids and stay-cool stainless steel handles. The cookware is not only efficient, but elegant enough for table service. Photo courtesy of Chantal by Lentrade, Inc.

up until she developed the cookware the majority of enameled cookware had either plastic or wooden handles and knobs. She designed the Chantal handles and knobs with a unique air pocket so that they remain cool. Stainless steel rims around both the lid and the pot prevent chipping. The bottom of the Chantal enamel-on-steel cookware is made of a heavy carbon steel core for even heat distribution.

"The handles of roasters always took up too much room in the oven, and I wanted to produce a larger capacity roaster, so I designed my roasters with comfortable handles on the sides," said Heida Thurlaw.

To complement the enamel-on-steel Chantal cookware Heida Thurlaw designed a Buffet Service Collection of stainless steel cookware which can also go from the stove to the table.

Glass Cookware

Heatproof glass cookware such as is produced by Corning can not only be used for cooking, but also for serving. It can be used in the microwave oven as well as a conventional oven. Since glass is non-porous, it does not absorb food flavors. Although many will tell you that you can take a glass cooking container from the freezer or refrigerator and place it in the oven, it is best to let the container and its contents warm up somewhat or place it in a cold oven. Rapid, extreme changes in temperature can crack glass cookware.

The best known glass cookware is Visions by Corning. It is amber in color and is available with DuPont SilverStone® non-stick surface in both pots and pans. You can sear and brown in it, as well as use it for slow cooking. The cookware can be used on the rangetop or in the microwave oven, and it is dishwasher safe. Visions is also available without the non-stick surface, and this cookware comes in the usual array of pots and pans as well as casseroles for oven baking.

The other well known name in glass cookware is Pyrex®, also a Corning product. In 1990 Pyrex® celebrated its 75th anniversary. Its casseroles, open bakers, pie plates, and loaf pans have provided baking and cooking pleasures for generations of cooks. Pyrex® is available in clear glass or in amber to coordinate with the Visions cookware.

Stainless Steel Cookware

Stainless steel cookware is very pretty to look at, but is known to be one of the poorest conductors of heat. If the pan is not well made it can also heat unevenly. Stainless steel is often combined with other metals to reduce any hot spot problems. These other metals are used as a "sandwich" at the bottom and/or sides of the pan to conduct heat. Stainless steel on the outside of the cookware looks attractive and on the inside it is non-reactive to acidic foods.

Cuisine Cookware's Steelpride line of pots and pans has some interesting innovations. There is a "Microcell" surface on the inside of the cookware instead of a chemical non-stick coating. This surface is a raised grid pattern on the inside bottom of the utensil which the manufacturer claims tends to trap small bubbles between the food and cooking surface, and keeps the food from touching the cooking surface. Consequently the pot comes clean with dishwashing detergent and a sponge. Part of the lid of Steelpride cookware has perforations so that you can use it as a colander. By simply twisting the lid's knob, the lid becomes solid. Part of the perforations can also be left exposed to release steam while cooking.

Stainless steel cookware is available in several gauges, the most popular being 18/8 and 18/10 in better cookware. There is great variety, not only in the type of utensils available in stainless steel, but also in price variations.

Chantal stainless steel cookware has a thick aluminum alloy disc attached to the bottom of each piece. It is then sandwiched with another layer of stainless steel for even heat distribution. This Chantal cookware also has stay-cool stainless steel handles and tempered glass lids.

On the other hand, Revere Ware®, a Corning product and a pioneer in stainless steel cookware, has a copper clad bottom for their pots and pans for even heat distribution and quick heating. Today there are three options in Revere Ware® — cookware with the copper clad bottom, cookware with an aluminum disk bottom, and cookware constructed of commercial gauge stainless steel with a copper disk sandwiched between the stainless steel bottom. The latter, an elegant looking product, is in the higher price category. Revere Ware® stainless steel open bakers with roasting racks, as

OVERVIEW OF COOKWARE MATERIALS AND THEIR USES

Material	Use
Aluminum	Large pots used for steaming
Anodized Aluminum	All-purpose cookware, also roasting pans and some bakeware
Cast Iron	Skillets for frying, griddles, Dutch ovens or similar oven pots, some casseroles
Ceramic	Baking dishes, particularly soufflé and gratin dishes, casseroles, quiche pans
Combination Metals	All-purpose cookware, including open bakers
Copper	Pots and pans for making sauces, sautéeing, and some gratin dishes
Enameled Cast Iron	Casseroles, pots for stews
Enameled Other Metals	All-purpose cookware, including roasters and bakers
Glass	Baking dishes, casseroles, pots and pans for stovetop use; also can be used in the microwave
Stainless Steel	All-purpose cookware, roasting pans, and soup pots

well as pie plates, loaf pans, and cake pans are also available.

Farberware, another pioneer in stainless steel cookware, uses a thick aluminum clad bottom in their heavy gauge pots and pans. The company recently introduced its Millennium Series of cookware, which is the first non-stick stainless steel cookware with a twenty-year warranty. The cookware has a triple coating of Excalibur, a revolutionary permanent non-stick coating reinforced with stainless steel. The Excalibur process consists of using molten stainless steel to adhere the non-stick finish which is baked on at 780 degrees F.

Farberware's Millennium Series of stainless steel cookware. Photo courtesy of Farberware, Inc.

The more expensive Cuisinart® Stainless Cookware has a thick copper disk sandwiched between two layers of stainless steel for quick and even heat distribution. This three-layer construction also helps to keep the bottoms of the cookware flat, and its vented handles minimize heat transfer.

PRESSURE COOKERS

In recent years the pressure cooker has been reinvented. It is safer, faster, and more versatile than the old models. Not only is the fear of pressure cooking gone, but home cooks have discovered that pressure cooking is a quick, economical, and nutritious way to prepare food. A pressure cooker cuts cooking time by about two-thirds and is a good way to cook less tender cuts of meat.

Pressure cookers come in various sizes — 4, 6, and 8 quarts. Most are made of heavy gauge stainless steel. However, Presto®, the first manufacturer of pressure cookers fifty years ago, produces them in both stainless steel and aluminum.

There are several unique safety features on the new pressure cookers. The Presto® models have a cover locking system, which allows pressure to build only when the cover is closed properly. The lock also prevents the cover from being opened until the pressure is safely reduced. The pressure regulator maintains proper cooking pressure automatically.

The Tefal pressure cooker also has a sensor activated lock system. Cuisinart® pressure cookers have a built-in valve in their covers with a red indicator light in the center. The light is marked with three rings to show the degree of pressure in the cooker. Another special feature of the Cuisinart pressure cooker is a red lever in the handle that allows the cook to quickly lower pressure without immersing the cooker in water. This pressure cooker also has a solid copper disc sandwich for even heat distribution.

By not sealing the lid, many models of pressure cookers can be used for conventional cooking. The large capacity of the pot is ideal for use as a steamer, stockpot, or pasta cooking pot.

Cuisinart®'s Quick Cuisine Pressure Cooker can prepare a variety of dishes. Photo courtesy of Cuisinarts, Inc.

BAKING EQUIPMENT NEEDS

Necessary	Optional Additions
13 by 9-inch cookie sheet	15½ by 10½ inch cookie sheet
13 by 9-inch cake pan	
8-inch square cake pan	Additional square cake pan
Two 9-inch round cake pans	Additional 9-inch round cake pan
9-inch round pie plate	10-inch round pie plate
Six compartment muffin pan	Additional muffin pan
9 by 5-inch loaf pan	Additional loaf pan
	2 mini loaf pans
10-inch tube pan	Bundt pan
9-inch springform pan	6-inch or 7½-inch and 10-inch springform pans
10-inch tart pan	8-inch tart pan
	Novelty cake pan, such as heart-shaped or Christmas tree-shaped
	French bread pans, if you bake that type of bread
	Kugelhopf pan

BAKING EQUIPMENT

The majority of the baking equipment — cookie or baking sheets, cake pans, bundt pans, muffin tins, pie plates, and tart pans — is constructed of anodized aluminum with a non-stick finish. These are not very expensive items. However, stainless baking equipment, which is preferred by the baking aficionados, is available from such manufacturers as Revere Ware by Corning and Chicago Metallic. These are very attractive and can be used for serving, and many also have a non-stick finish.

Heatproof glass dishes also make good baking pans and can be used for table service. These do not have a non-stick finish and need to be greased before using to avoid the baked goods adhering to the surface. It is recommended that the oven temperature be lowered by 25 degrees when baking in glass utensils.

The preceding is a list of basic baking equipment commonly used. However, you may add or subtract from the list depending on your individual needs. I have listed the items that I think are necessary and those that are optional. The tart and springform pans should have removable rims for easy serving.

To complete any baking equipment there should be mixing bowls, measuring cups and measuring spoons, and one or two spatulas. The bowls and cups can be stainless steel, tempered glass, or heavy duty plastic. Some bowls are also available in ceramic. Other kitchen gadgets which are also used in cooking can be used in baking (see list on page 156).

KITCHEN KNIVES

Kitchen knives are of prime importance in cooking. They should be solidly constructed and for best performance should be kept sharp. Dull knives are not only useless, but can be dangerous. Proper storage of knives is important to maintain their sharpness. They should be stored in individual slots in a knife holder, placed either in a kitchen drawer, mounted on the wall, or set on the countertop.

Properly functioning kitchen knives are constructed of steel. Carbon steel provides the sharpest edges for knives, but tends to pit and discolor easily when used with acidic foods. Stainless steel knives are non-reactive and consequently stay clean looking, but they are hard and therefore more difficult to sharpen. The ideal knives are made of high-carbon steel which holds a sharp edge and is non-reactive.

Every kitchen should have three basic knives,

and additional ones are the option of the cook. Also to be considered when selecting a knife is how it feels in your hand. Is it hard to hold so that it makes cutting difficult? Is the handle too long to get good leverage for cutting? The following is a list of basic knives and optional ones you can add, depending on your needs. If there are two cooks in your family you may want an additional knife for certain preparation tasks.

Basic Knives

Paring knife, 3 to 4 inches long, for trimming fruits and vegetables and for cutting small pieces of food.

Chef's knife, 9 to 12 inches long, for slicing larger foods, including some meats.

Serrated knife, 10 to 12 inches long, for slicing bread and other soft foods, such as tomatoes. This knife should not be carbon steel because acidic fruits and vegetables will discolor it.

Optional Knives

Utility knife, 6 to 8 inches long, for medium slicing jobs.

Carving knife, 10 to 12 inches long, for carving meats and poultry.

A boning knife, 6 to 8 inches long, with an indented blade for cutting around bones. These are available both rigid and flexible. If you do a lot of meat and fish preparation at home it is nice to have both — the rigid one for meats, and the flexible one for fish and poultry.

Cleaver for chopping vegetables. A tool used in Oriental cooking, but one to be worked with carefully so that you do not chop your fingers.

KITCHEN GADGETS

There is a myriad of kitchen gadgets available. It would be impossible to describe every one of them because each cook has her own preferences in small kitchen equipment that is used in food

NECESSARY KITCHEN TOOLS

Cake tester
Tongs
Measuring spoons
Measuring cups
Rolling pin
Cooling racks for baked
 goods
Pastry brush
Hand juicer
Hand grater
Wide and narrow
 spatulas
Mixing spoons
Flour sifter
Garlic press
Vegetable peeler
Cutting board
Potato ricer, if you do
 not have a hand mixer
 or food processor
Pot-edge strainer
Salad spinner
Fruit ripener
Scale
Whisk
Wooden spoons
Pasta rake
Gravy separator
Pastry blender
Strainer

OPTIONAL KITCHEN TOOLS

Ice cream scoop
Funnel
Pastry scooper, if you bake a lot of cakes
Egg ring
Pouring pitcher for batters
Apple slicer
Nut chopper
Yeast thermometer, if you bake yeast doughs
Candy thermometer, if you make candy
Zucchini corer
Two-headed tenderizer
Battery operated flour sifter
Nutmeg grater
Mortar and pestle
Strawberry huller
Honey dipper
Ravioli tray
Savarin mold
Brioche mold
Croissant cutter
Egg slicer
Shrimp cleaner
Pastry bags and tubes
Pastry wheel
Goose feather pastry brush
Flan form
Melon baller
Butter molds

preparation. I took a survey of several working cooks to determine which gadgets they used frequently and which they used infrequently. All of the women surveyed do a variety of cooking from quick and easy to formal dinner parties. They also do a fair amount of baking.

The options as well as the necessities on the following list can be varied to suit your individual needs. This survey is based on the consensus of the most frequently used and least frequently used items.

Since kitchen gadgets are not expensive items, they can be purchased as impulse items as your cooking needs change. I love shopping for kitchen gadgets and am always fascinated with the huge selection available.

Appendix

This Appendix includes, under each segment of the kitchen, a brief summary of points to remember when planning your own project. In addition, there is a checklist of questions on various aspects of the kitchen. For further information, you will want to refer back to individual chapters in the main part of the text relating to a specific subject.

It is wise to keep a notebook and, as you are working in your kitchen, list your likes and dislikes as well as any improvements you would like to make in your current kitchen. You should also make notes on various appliance features as you do your preliminary shopping.

At current building rates, kitchen remodeling as well as kitchen building costs about $100 to $120 per square foot for the average kitchen. The actual cost will depend on how extensive the structural changes are, particularly the amount of plumbing and electrical work necessary. In addition to the building estimate, you should add any appliance costs and cabinet costs. According to the survey taken of kitchen planners by the National Kitchen and Bath Association, the average cost of kitchen remodeling in 1990 was $17,500.

The structural and architectural aspects of a home can pose limitations on remodeling or expansion of a kitchen. In addition to the placement of major appliances, there might also be structural limitations on the installation of a ventilation hood over the cooking area. The same may also be true for a downdraft ventilation system. Thus, it is always a good idea to check your existing house plans before contemplating any changes in your kitchen.

THE STRUCTURE OF THE KITCHEN

Traffic flow and the space between work centers are important considerations in planning your kitchen. If there is more than one cook in the family, space and facilities should be provided for each cook. If the kitchen incorporates an eating area, there should be sufficient space surrounding it for easy traffic flow. Combining the kitchen with the family room can create a more luxurious feeling and coordinate family activities with those of the cook.

In planning any kitchen you should consider distinct areas for food preparation, cooking, and cleanup. These should be within easy access of each other and form a work triangle. However, built-in ovens typically are not included in this basic triangle. Also, the basic triangle does not include specialty areas, such as a baking area, hospitality area, or planning area.

Although there are many kitchen plans, they usually fall into basic categories — the one wall kitchen, the galley kitchen. the L-shaped kitchen, and the U-shaped kitchen. Peninsulas and islands add additional work space and informal eating space to many kitchens.

The following questions will help you formulate plans for your kitchen:

1. What size kitchen do you need? What size can you afford — 100 to 150 square feet, 150 to 300 square feet, 300 to 400 square feet, over 400 square feet?

2. Of the four kitchen configurations, which is your existing kitchen? If you are planning to remodel or build a new kitchen which type of plan do you prefer? Which is feasible?

3. How many cooks are there in your family? Do teenagers prepare their own snacks and meals?

4. Do you have an eating area in your kitchen? If not, do you want to add one?

5. Do you want to open your kitchen into an existing family room?

6. Do you do your meal planning in the kitchen? Do you occasionally do some of the family bookkeeping in the kitchen? If so, do you have or want a planning center? Do you have a telephone in your kitchen and a message center in a convenient place?

7. Do you have distinct work areas in your kitchen for food preparation, for cooking, and for cleanup? Do these areas form a comfortable triangle? Do you have sufficient counter space in each work area and next to the refrigerator, cooktop, ovens, and sink?

8. Do you want a baking center in your kitchen?

9. Do you want a hospitality center for drink preparation?

10. In remodeling your existing kitchen, will electrical, gas, water, and sewer connections have to be altered? Is it feasible to do so? Is it feasible to move windows, walls, doors, and make other structural changes that you desire? Can the necessary ventilation be installed?

In the survey taken by the National Kitchen and Bath Association (NKBA), 7% of those surveyed preferred a kitchen of 150 square feet, 69% preferred a kitchen of 150 to 300 square feet, 18% preferred a kitchen of 300 to 400 square feet and 6% preferred one of over 400 square feet. In the same survey, 31% of the kitchens were used by multiple cooks, 47% had a center island, 33% had a peninsula, and 34% had a planning center.

MAJOR APPLIANCES

The type and diversity of cooking appliances in the kitchen are determined by several factors. The style of cooking is a major factor in deciding the type of appliances you want in your kitchen. If you prepare a great number of quick meals your emphasis on major cooking appliances will be on microwave ovens, cooktops (either in a range or separate), and possibly indoor grills. Your option in cooktops will probably be gas or the faster heating electric elements.

On the other hand, if you like to do a lot of baking, casserole cookery, and slow roasting of meats, you will probably want two ovens — one being a microwave-convection combination.

Another consideration in planning major cooking appliances for your kitchen is space and the structural aspects of your home. Often, structural changes are necessary to provide an area for a built-in oven or ovens and counters. Cabinets will need to be altered to accommodate a built-in cooktop.

If space limitations do not permit the separate cooktop and built-in ovens, the free-standing and drop-in ranges have many of the features present in built-ins. If you have space for only one built-in oven, the drop-in range can provide a second one.

The budget is another consideration in either adding or replacing major cooking appliances. A drop-in range with a self-cleaning oven is $500 to $600. An eye-level free-standing range with two ovens starts at $1200 and ranges up to $7000 for the four oven AGA stove. Of course, there are many options in between. The price of a built-in cooktop ranges from $250 to $1200 depending on its amenities. A Jenn-Air induction cooktop ranges from

$1500 to $2000 and a separate built-in Jenn-Air grill is $250 to $350.

Refrigerator/freezers also depend on the cooking and eating styles of the individual household. The size of the family will help determine the size of the refrigerator. If you food shop frequently you will want a unit with more refrigerator space than the person who shops every two or three weeks and buys a lot of frozen foods or freezes a lot of meats. The latter will be more interested in freezer space. How often you use ice cubes will help determine whether you want an in-the-door ice dispenser.

The type of refrigeration unit you have is also determined by the space allowed for it — whether it is a side-by-side unit or one of the new built-ins. If you change the width or depth of your refrigerator you may also have to make changes in the kitchen cabinets. There are various configurations of refrigerator/freezers as well as storage space within the units.

A 22 cubic foot refrigerator can range in cost from $550 to $1100, depending on its amenities. A side-by-side 30 cubic foot unit with an ice dispenser in the door is $1200 to $1300. A 22 cubic foot refrigerator with the freezer on the bottom ranges $800 to $900. An under-the-counter or bar refrigerator varies from $200 to $700.

The cleanup area is centered around the sink and usually includes a dishwasher. Garbage disposals and trash compactors are also included in this area. Sinks come in a variety of configurations from single to double to triple bowls, as well as in a variety of materials. Faucets, too, have many options.

Sinks range in cost from $400 to $1200 and faucets range from $150 to $500. Dishwashers run from $300 to $800; trash compactors $300 to $400; garbage disposals are $200 to $400.

The following questions will help formulate your major appliance needs:

1. What type of cooking do you usually do? Quick, microwave, stir-frying, sautéeing and steaming, oven meals, combination of stovetop and oven cooking? Have you included a suitable appliance for each?

2. Do you buy a lot of packaged and frozen foods to prepare in the microwave oven? Is your microwave oven of sufficient size and does it have suitable features? Have you planned for sufficient freezer space for frozen foods?

3. Do other members of your family do a significant amount of cooking? If so, what are their cooking preferences? Has adequate counter and storage space been provided? Are additional appliances needed?

4. Do the teenagers in your household prepare quick meals or snacks on their own? If so, what type of additional equipment and/or space do they require?

5. Do you like to grill or barbecue? Can you fit a separate indoor grill into your budget? Is there sufficient counter space for it?

6. Does a member of the family have a cooking specialty that requires unusual cooking equipment? What type of equipment?

7. Do you prefer gas or electric cooking appliances? Are the proper energy and exhaust connections available for your preference? If not, can they be provided?

8. Do you often prepare breakfast or brunch that would include pancakes for a crowd? Is your cooktop equipped with a suitable griddle?

9. What is your style of entertaining? Do you entertain often? Are your dinner parties formal multi-course ones or informal, casual, and often buffet-type meals? Do you have sufficient counter space for serving? Do you have freezer space for casseroles and frozen desserts? Would a separate salad preparation area be advisable?

10. If you plan to install a new cooktop, will there be proper ventilation?

11. How often do you grocery shop — daily, once a week, every two or three weeks?

12. Is your present refrigerator large enough to accommodate your food purchases? If not, what size will you need? Do you have sufficient freezer space?

13. If you are purchasing a new refrigerator, what combination of features do you want?

14. Do you need a hospitality area in the kitchen? Do you need a bar sink? Do you need an under-the-counter refrigerator for this area?

15. If you are changing your sink, what type and material best suit your needs and decor?

16. Is a special kitchen faucet high on your priority list? How about an instant hot water attachment?

17. Do you need a dishwasher? What features do you desire?

18. Does a garbage disposal and/or trash compactor fit within your budget?

According to the NKBA survey 78% of the new and remodeled kitchens in 1990 have built-in appliances, while 3½% have free-standing ones. The rest of the kitchens have a combination of free-standing and built-ins. Ninety-one percent of the kitchens have a microwave oven; 83% a garbage disposal; 38% a trash compactor; and 22% have more than one sink in the kitchen.

KITCHEN CABINETS, MATERIALS, AND DECORATION

There is a great variety in style as well as storage configurations available in today's kitchen cabinets. Kitchen cabinets are available in either stock modules, semi-custom, or custom built. There are many special cabinets available for specific storage needs. The majority of their surfaces are either wood or laminates.

The materials available for use in a kitchen include tile, wood, marble, granite, laminates, solid surfaces, paint, and wallpaper. Each has its own advantages or disadvantages from the standpoint of use, decor, and cost. The selection of materials often determines the overall decor of the kitchen. A variety of materials can be combined for different purposes and decors.

The following questions will help you formulate your cabinet and kitchen material needs:

1. Are you planning new kitchen cabinets? If so, do you prefer wood or laminates? If wood, what type of wood and what shade of stain; or do you prefer painted wood cabinets?

2. Do you have specific storage needs? Do you store a lot of canned goods and soft drinks? Are you limited for storage space and could use a pantry with storage in the doors as well as swing-out shelves? Is there room for a walk-in pantry?

3. Do you store your small appliances in a cabinet or on the counter? Would you group your food preparation appliances together in an appliance garage?

4. Do you have or want a baking center with a specially designed cabinet for a large stand-alone mixer?

5. Can corner cabinets be used to contain lazy Susans?

6. What type of floor do you prefer in the kitchen? Do you prefer the elegant look although hard feel of ceramic tile, or the softer look and more comfortable feel of vinyl?

7. What type of countertop do you prefer — stain resistant ceramic tile or granite, or the continuous look of solid surface, or the less expensive laminates? Or would you like a combination of countertop materials for specific work areas?

8. What will be the style of your new kitchen? Does it coordinate with the rest of the house or with an adjoining family room? What materials and decor will best tie your kitchen into the adjoining rooms of the house?

9. Do you have a decorating theme for your kitchen? Do you have collectibles that you would like to display in your kitchen? What fixtures or shelves have you included to provide for these decorative items?

According to the NKBA survey, 71% of all kitchens built or remodeled in the past year were traditional, with 20% being European in styling. The remaining 8% were French provincial or other styles. Only 14% of the cabinets were stock items, 22% were semi-custom, and 64% were custom cabinets. Eighty-seven percent of the cabinets were wood, with only 12% being laminates. The rest were stainless steel or free-standing storage units. The majority of the wooden cabinets were oak.

Special storage units were the norm, not the exception, in kitchen cabinets. Ninety-two percent of the kitchens had lazy Susans, 57% had appliance garages, 4% had recycling bins, 49% had spice racks, 54% had pantries, 84% had pull-out shelves, 11% had cutting boards, 28% had pull-out waste baskets, 59% had tilt-down sink fronts, 37% had cutlery dividers, 17% had pot racks, and 39% had a video-stereo-TV center.

Laminates were the most popular countertops representing 56% of the total. Thirty-two percent had solid surface countertops, 9% had tile, and 1% had granite. For floors, 67% preferred vinyl, 24% ceramic tile, 8% wood, and 1% carpet. Wallpaper and paint for the walls were the most popular choices among kitchen owners with 56% opting for wallpaper and 40% for paint, while 4% installed ceramic tile. The overall colors in the kitchens ranged from white for 42%, to almond for 21%, to wood tones for 27%, and pastels for 7%. The other 3% had various bright colors.

SMALL APPLIANCES, COOKWARE, AND GADGETS

There is a myriad of small appliances, cookware, and kitchen gadgets available. New appliances, new cookware, and more gadgets are constantly appearing on the market. For example, if you do not like deep-fried foods, there is no reason to own a deep-fryer. On the other hand, if you like espresso coffee, you might consider an espresso machine. If you want to use your cooking utensils as serving dishes, you will be interested in the enamel-steel, stainless steel, or heatproof glass cookware.

Kitchen gadgets are also a matter of preference, but certain ones such as measuring cups and spoons and a vegetable peeler are a must.

No set of questions could suggest what you need in the above items. So, have fun shopping for them. My only advice is to make sure you provide enough storage space for them, particularly if, like me, you do not want to clutter your countertops with kitchen appliances and gadgets.

MANUFACTURERS

The manufacturers listed on the following pages have contributed information and photographs for this book. This list is by no means a complete one of the appliance, cabinet, and kitchen material manufacturers. It merely reflects those whose information I used. The resources are listed by categories.

MANUFACTURERS' ADDRESSES

Antique Stoves

Bryant Stove Works
R.F.D. 2, Box 2048
Thorndike, ME 04986
(207) 568-3365

Cumberland General Store
Rte. 3
Crossville, TN 38555
Outside TN: (800) 334-4640
In TN (216) 484-8481

Elmira Stove Works
22 Church Street
West Elmira, Ontario N3B 1M3, Canada
(519) 669-5103

The Antique Stove Association
414 N. Main St.
Monticello, IN 47960

Major Appliances

Admiral Division Headquarters
1701 E. Woodfield Road
Schaumburg, IL 60196
(312) 884-2600

Amana Refrigeration, Inc.
Amana, Iowa 52204
(319) 622-5511

AGA Cookers
R.F.D. 1, Box 477
Stowe, VT 05672
(802) 253-9729

Caloric Corp.
403 N. Main Street
Topton, PA 19562
(215) 682-4211

Dacor
950 S. Raymond Ave.
Pasadena, CA 91105
(213) 682-2803

Gaggenau USA Corp.
5 Commonwealth Avenue
Woburn, MA 01801
(617) 938-1655

Garland Commercial Industries
185 E. South St.
Freeland, PA 18224
(717) 636-1000

General Electric
Louisville, KY 40225
(800) 626-2000

Jenn-Air
3035 Shadeland
Indianapolis, IN 46226
(317) 545-2271

KitchenAid, Inc.
701 Main Street
St. Joseph, MI 49085
(616) 472-3372

Maytag Co.
1 Dependability Square
Newton, Iowa 50208
(515) 792-7000

Modern Maid Company
403 N. Main Street
Topton, PA 19562
(215) 682-4211

Panasonic
1 Panasonic Way
Secaucus, NJ 07094
(201) 348-7000

Sub-Zero Freezer Company
P.O. Box 4130
Madison, WI 53711
(608) 271-2233

Thermador
5119 District Boulevard
Los Angeles, CA 90040
(213) 562-1133

Toshiba America, Inc.
82 Totowa Road
Wayne, NJ 07470
(201) 628-8000

Traulsen & Co., Inc.
114-02 15th Avenue
College Point, NY 11356
(718) 463-9000

WCI Appliance Group
WCI Major Appliance Center
300 Phillipi Road
Columbus, OH 43228

    Gibson Appliances
    (800) 458-1445

    Whirlpool Corp.
    2000 M63 North
    Benton Harbor, MI 49022
    (800) 253-1301

    Frigidaire
    6000 Perimeter Drive
    Dublin, OH 43017
    (800) 451-7007

Cabinets

Alno Kitchen Cabinets, Inc.
385 Bellevue Drive
Newark, DE 19713
(302) 366-8592

Kraft Maid Cabinetry, Inc.
16052 Industrial Parkway
P.O. Box 1055
Middlefield, OH 44062
(216) 632-5333

Merillat Industries, Inc.
5353 W. U.S. 223
P.O. Box 1946
Adrain, MI 49221
(517) 263-0771

Quaker Maid
State Route 61
Leesport, PA 19533
(215) 926-3011

Wood-Mode Cabinetry
1 Second Street
Kreamer, PA 17833
(717) 374-2711

Plumbing Fixtures and Ventilation Equipment

Abbaka
435 23rd Street
San Francisco, CA 94107
(415) 648-7210

Broan Manufacturing Co. Inc.
Hartford, WI 53027
(414) 673-4340

The Elkay Manufacturing Company
2222 Camden Court
Oak Brook, IL 60521
(312) 574-8484

Franke, Inc.
P.O. Box 428
Hatfield, PA 19440
(800) 626-5771

Gaggenau USA Corp.
5 Commonwealth Avenue
Woburn, MA 01801
(617) 938-1655

Grohe America, Inc.
900 Lively Boulevard
Wood Dale, IL 60191
(312) 350-2600

The Kohler Company
444 Highland Drive
Kohler, WI 53044
(414) 457-4441

Vance Industries,Inc.
7401 W. Wilson Avenue
Chicago, Ill 60656
(708) 867-6000

Surface Materials — Floors and Countertops

Armstrong World Industries, Inc.
P. O. Box 3001
Lancaster, PA 19446
(215) 855-1111

Avonite
12836 Arroyo Street
Sylmar, CA 91342
(800) AVONITE

E.I. Dupont de Nemours & Co.
Corian Building Products
1007 Market Street
Wilmington, DE 19898
(302) 774-6602
or (800) 441-7515

Formica Corp.
One Stanford Road
P.O. Box 338
Piscataway, NJ 08854
(201) 469-1555

Ralph Wilson Plastics Co.
600 General Bruce Drive
Temple, TX 76501
(800) 433-3222

Small Appliances

American Harvest
4064 Peavy Road
Chaska, MN 55318
(612) 448-4400
or (800) 624-2949

Broan Inc.
66 Broadway, Route 1
Lynnfield, MA 01940
(617) 596-7350

Cuisinart, Inc.
1 Cummings Point Road
Stamford, CT 06904
(203) 351-9000

DeLonghi America, Inc.
625 Washington Avenue
Carlstadt, NJ 07072
(201) 507-1110

Emile Henry International
Kingswood Court
Foxrock, Dublin 18 Ireland
(353) 195-4511

Farberware, Inc.
1500 Bassett Avenue
Bronx, NY 10461
(212) 863-8000

Hitachi Sales Corp. of America
401 W. Artesia Blvd.
Compton, CA 90220
(213) 537-8383

KitchenAid, Inc.
701 Main Street
St. Joseph, MI 49085
(616) 982-4537

Robert Krups, North America
7 Reuten Drive
Closter, NJ 07624
(201) 767-5500

Moulinex Appliances Inc.
10 Sims Crescent
Richmond Hill, Ontario L4B 1K9 Canada
(416) 881-6514

National Presto Industries, Inc.
3925 N. Hastings Way
Eau Claire, WI 54703
(715) 839-2121

Panasonic
1 Panasonic Way
Secaucus, NJ 07094
(201) 348-7000

Proctor-Silex
4421 Waterfront Drive
Glen Allen, VA 23060
(804) 273-9777

Salton/Maxim Housewares Group
550 Business Center Drive
Mt. Prospect, IL 60056
(312) 803-4600

Sunbeam Appliance Company
8989 N. Deerwood Drive, Ste. 250
Brown Deer, WI 53223
(414) 362-7120

Toastmaster, Inc.
1801 N. Stadium Blvd.
Columbia, MO 65202
(314) 445-8666

The West Bend Company
400 Washington Street
West Bend, WI 53095
(414) 334-2311

Zojirushi America Corporation
5628 Bandini Boulevard
Bell, CA 90201
(213) 264-6270

Cookware

Chantal by Lentrade, Inc.
2030 W. Sam Houston Parkway
Houston, TX 77043
(713) 467-9949

Chicago Metallic
800 Ela Road
Lake Zurich, IL 60047
(708) 438-3400

Crown Corning®/Revere®
South Sherman Street
P.O. Box 250
Clinton, IL 61727
(217) 935-7200

Le Creuset
P.O. Box 575
River Road
Yemassee, SC 29945
(800) 589-6211

Farberware, Inc.
1500 Bassett Avenue
Bronx, NY 10461
(212) 863-8000

Lodge Manufacturing Company
Box 380
6th Street at Railroad Avenue
South Pittsburgh, TN 37380
(615) 837-7181

Regal Ware, Inc.
1675 Reigle Drive
Kewaskum, WI 53040
(414) 626-2121

T-Fal Corporation
208 Passaic Avenue
Fairfield, NJ 07006
(201) 575-1060

Wearever/Member of Newell Group
P.O. Box 1330
Manitowoc, WI 54221
(414) 684-4421

Index